THE FUN HOUSE

BY

LYNDA BARRY

PERENNIAL LIBRARY

HARPER & ROW, PUBLISHERS
—NEW YORK—

CAMBRIDGE, PHILADELPHIA, SAN FRANCISCO, WASHINGTON, LONDON, MEXICO CITY, SÃO PAULO, SINGAPORE, SYDNEY

THE SUBSTITUTE

By LYNDA RINGA DINGA DING DANG BARRY © 1987

OUR USUAL TEACHER HAD ACTUALLY QUIT BECAUSE OF US. BECAUSE OUR MOST ROTTENEST PERSON, NAME OF JOHN BAILEY, KICKED HER LEGS AND YELLED "YOU'RE NOT THE BOSS OF ME!" MISS ANASLY STARTED CRYING AND WALKED OUT. THEN WE HEARD SHE HAD TO MOVE TO NORTH DAKOTA WHERE CHILDREN HAVE BETTER RESPECT.

I AM MISS BEVENS,

YOUR SUBSTITUTE.

MISS BEVENS WAS OUR MAIN PUNISHMENT FOR BEING SUCH A AWFUL CLASS. SHE HAD THIS CRUSTY PITCH PIPE WHICH SHE WOULD BLOW, THEN MAKE US SING THE WORST SONGS YOU EVER HEARD IN YOUR LIFE. ALSO SHE HAD A BIG POINTY BOSOM AND FAKE TEETH THAT FLIPPED AROUND.

♪ "SOMEONE" IS NOT PAYING AT-TEN-TION... ♪

CLICK CLICK CLICK CLICK

SHE ALSO HAD A SPECIAL SMELL, A PERFUME SMELL THAT PRACTICALLY CHOKED YOUR HEAD OFF WHEN SHE WAS BY YOU. AND SHE DIDN'T EVEN CARE IF YOU SAW HER EAT. DURING A MATH TEST WE SAW HER TRY TO EAT A CHICKEN LEG. EVERYONE GOT AT LEAST MINUS 8 ON THAT MATH TEST.

ON A FRIDAY MISS BEVENS TOLD US THE SCHOOL HAD GOT US A PERMANENT TEACHER, SO THIS WAS HER LAST DAY. SHE ASKED US FOR A SPECIAL FAVOR WHICH WAS TO SING HER HER FAVORITE SONG OF "JOHN BROWN'S BODY LIES A MOLDERING IN THE GRAVE" WE STOOD UP AND SANG IT AND IF WE HATED HER SO MUCH HOW COME A LOT OF US STARTED CRYING?

READY? HERE'S OUR NOTE...

SCIENCE

BY LYNDA GOLF BALL BARRY ©1987

MRS. BROGAN SAID SMOKING IS BAD ENOUGH, BUT TEACHING A GRASSHOPPER TO SMOKE IS TOTAL CRUELTY TO ANIMALS. ERNIE SAID IT'S NOT A REAL CIGAR BUT MRS. BROGAN MADE HIM LET THE TALENTED BRUCE LEE JR. GO. AT RECESS WE SADLY WATCHED IT JUMP THROUGH THE FENCE AND INTO THE STICKERS.

I KNOW YOU'RE UPSET NOW ERNEST, BUT ONE DAY YOU'LL THANK ME. YOU'LL SAY "BY GOLLY, MRS. BROGAN WAS THE BEST TEACHER I EVER HAD!" AND YOU'LL WANT TO SEND ME FLOWERS.

MRS. BROGAN SAT AT HER DESK AND ASKED US TO THINK ABOUT WHAT VALUABLE LESSON HAD WE LEARNED THAT DAY. THE ANSWER WAS "WHAT EVER YOU DO, NEVER SHOW NOTHING GOOD TO MRS. BROGAN."

BORN FREEE AS FREE AS THE WIND BLOWS...

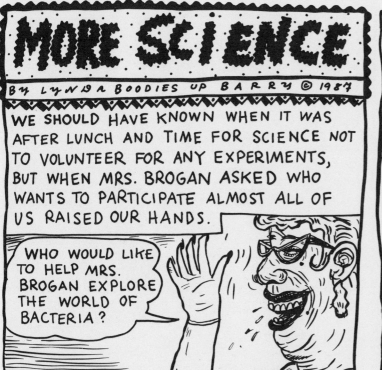

MORE SCIENCE

BY LYNDA BOODIES UP BARRY © 1987

WE SHOULD HAVE KNOWN WHEN IT WAS AFTER LUNCH AND TIME FOR SCIENCE NOT TO VOLUNTEER FOR ANY EXPERIMENTS, BUT WHEN MRS. BROGAN ASKED WHO WANTS TO PARTICIPATE ALMOST ALL OF US RAISED OUR HANDS.

WHO WOULD LIKE TO HELP MRS. BROGAN EXPLORE THE WORLD OF BACTERIA?

OUT OF ALL THE CLASS SHE PICKED MARCIE WHO WAS JUST A REGULAR GIRL WITH A REGULAR AMOUNT OF FRIENDS UNTIL MRS BROGAN ASKED MARCIE TO COUGH ON THE CLEAR JELLO IN THE PETRIE DISH.

THIS EXPERIMENT WILL SHOW HOW TINY INVISIBLE GERMS ARE EVERYWHERE IN MARCIE'S MOUTH.

MRS. BROGAN WROTE MARCIE'S NAME ON THE PETRIE DISH AND SIX DAYS LATER THERE WAS A HUNKING WAD OF BLUE MOLD GROWING ALL OVER THAT JELLO. THAT MOLD ALTERED MARCIE'S SOCIAL STATUS FOR THE NEXT FIVE YEARS.

GO ON...

WELL, THEY CALLED ME "MOLD MOUTH" AFTER THAT, DR., FOR YEARS. MRS. BROGAN IS LONG DEAD BUT I STILL HAVE VIVID FANTASIES OF SHOVING THAT PETRIE DISH DOWN HER THROAT.

IT IS MY OBSESSION.

WHEN MRS. BROGAN ASKED US WHAT WE HAD LEARNED FROM THIS EXPERIMENT I GUESS IT WAS "DON'T COUGH ON JELLO"

COME ON NOW!

VALUABLE CLASS TIME IS BEING WASTED! I NEED TWO VOLUNTEERS FOR OUR "MYSTERIES OF SALIVA" DISPLAY.

NOBODY?

NOBODY WANTS TO EXPERIENCE THE WONDERS OF SCIENCE WITH MRS. BROGAN?

THE PIDGEON

STORY BY BILL S. OVER DINNER • EXAGGERATION BY L. BARRY © 88

ONE WEIRD THING ABOUT THE NEW KID BILL WAS HIS PIDGEON THAT CAME TO SCHOOL WITH HIM EVERY DAY, FLYING UP THE HILL AND SITTING NO MATTER WHAT IN THE ONE MAIN TREE BY THE LUNCHROOM. WHEN YOU WOULD SHARPEN YOUR PENCIL YOU COULD ALWAYS SEE THAT BIRD AND YOU WOULD LOOK AT THE BIRD, THEN LOOK AT BILL, THEN LOOK AT THE BIRD.

THIS SHARPENER IS A TOOL NOT A TOY

ALL OF THE GIRLS AUTOMATICALLY WANTED TO BE BILL'S GIRLFRIEND BECAUSE OF THE PIDGEON AND ALL OF THE BOYS AUTOMATICALLY STARTED THROWING ROCKS AT IT WHEN NO ONE WAS LOOKING. SOMEONE SAID THE SPIRIT OF BILL'S DEAD GRANDMA WAS IN THE BIRD SO QUIT THROWING ROCKS. THEN IT TURNED OUT BILL'S GRANDMA WASN'T EVEN DEAD. WHEN THE THREE O'CLOCK BELL RANG THE BIRD ALWAYS FLEW DOWN THE HILL, STOPPING ON TELE-PHONE POLES, WAITING FOR BILL TO CATCH UP.

WHEN OUR SCHOOL ENTERED INTO THE COUNTY SCIENCE FAIR NATURALLY WE ALL WANTED BILL'S PIDGEON TO BE THE PROJECT. EVEN THE TEACHER DID, EVEN THE PRINCIPAL DID, MAN, EVEN THE JANITORS DID. ALL OF A SUDDEN THE SUBJECT OF PIDGEONS WAS OUR MAIN THING. WE READ STUFF ABOUT THEM AND DREW THEIR PICTURES AND YOU NAME IT. THE IDEA WAS THE PIDGEON WOULD JUST FLY BY ITSELF TO THE SCIENCE FAIR WITH A MESSAGE AND MAKE THE WHOLE COUNTY PRACTICALLY FAINT FROM AMAZEMENT.

BILL DIDN'T TELL NO ONE THAT HE HAD TO WALK ALL THE WAY FIVE MILES TO THE FAIR BECAUSE PIDGEONS CAN'T FOLLOW, FOR EXAMPLE, A CAR. HE TOLD HIS MOM HE WAS GETTING A RIDE WITH OUR TEACHER. BY THE TIME HE GOT THERE IT WAS TOO LATE. FIRST PRIZE ALREADY WENT TO A GIRL WHO COULD MAKE WATER BOIL IN SOME DUMB WAY. WE WERE ALL MAD ESPECIALLY BILL'S MOM WHO MADE HIM RIDE BACK HOME IN THE CAR SAYING SHE DIDN'T GIVE A DAMN ABOUT THAT BIRD, HOW DARE HER SON LIE TO HER, AND THAT DAMN BIRD COULD FIND ITS OWN WAY BACK. WELL OF COURSE IT NEVER DID.

School Pictures

BY LYNDA "TOO WEAK TO FIGHT IT" BARRY

OUR TEACHER GIVE US GOOD WARNING. ON TOMORROW IS GOING TO BE SCHOOL PICTURES TIME. EVERYBODY EXITED. WE GO HOME AND PRACTICE OUR MISS AMERICA IN THE MIRROR. THE BOYS GO GET A HAIR CUT.

GIVE IT UP, MAN. YOU GONNA BREAK THAT CAMERA

SHUT UP SKITCH HEAD.

EVERYBODY TRY TO LOOK SOMEHOW EXTRA GOOD FOR THAT PICTURE, KNOWN AS DOING A BEAUTY EXPERIMENT. ONE GIRL WANTED A TAN AND USE HER MAMA'S SUNLAMP AND COME TO SCHOOL WITH A TOTALLY FUNKY HEAD ALL BURNT UP LIKE A SCIENCE PROJECT. ANOTHER GIRL TO STRAIGHTEN HER HAIR, WRAP HER HEAD WITH SPRAINED ANKLE BANDAGES LIKE A BANDAID MUMMY. SHE COME TO SCHOOL BUT THE BANDAGE MARKS STAY ON HER FACE ALL DAY.

AT RECESS NO ONE HARDLY MOVES WILD SO THEY WON'T MESS UP HOW THEY LOOK. NO GIRLS GO ON THE MONKEY BARS. NO BOYS RUNNING AND YELLING. ABOUT YOUR ONLY CHOICE OF A PLAY WAS SPITTING CONTEST. RIGHT AFTER RECESS WAS THE PICTURES.

WE ALL LINE UP BY THE ALPHABET AND WE ARE ALL IN LINE EXCEPT DEAN ARGESON. HE STILL AT HIS DESK AND THE REASON IS HIS BIG BLACK EYE. HE DIDN'T GET THAT EYE FROM FALLING OVER LIKE HE SAID. ANYBODY WOULD KNOW WHO GIVE HIM THAT WITH A DADDY DRUNK ALL THE TIME. SO THERES NO PICTURE OF DEAN BUT THAT'S NORMAL.

ART PROJECT

BY LYNDA "AWARENESS" BARRY © 1987

WHEN IT CAME TIME FOR AN ART PERIOD THE FIRST THING MRS. BROGAN DID WAS HAND OUT PAPER PLATES. PAPER PLATES FOR SKELETONS, PUMPKINS, TURKEYS, CHRISTMAS DECORATIONS, GEORGE WASHINGTON-HEADS, VALENTINES, THE WHOLE YEAR.

"PUMPKY" "TOMMY"

"SPOOKY" BY DUANE

BY DUANE

"HEARTY" "FROSTY"

"GLOBEY"

BEFORE WE WOULD BEGIN OUR PROJECTS MRS. BROGAN WOULD TELL US TO WORK CAREFULLY BECAUSE SHE WAS NOT MADE OUT OF PAPER PLATES. NO ONE IN OUR CLASS DOUBTED THIS, BUT SHE ALWAYS SAID IT.

SINCE THIS IS ART, FEEL FREE TO BE CREATIVE. MRS. BROGAN'S WAY IS NOT THE ONLY WAY TO DO THINGS! BUT REMEMBER, IF YOU USE YOUR IMAGINATION AND YOUR PROJECT IS RUINED...... YOU WILL GET A BAD GRADE WHICH WILL GO ON YOUR PERMANENT FILE WHICH WILL FOLLOW YOU FOR THE REST OF YOUR LIFE!

ANY QUESTIONS?

ONE TIME WHEN WE WERE MAKING THE NIÑA, THE PINTA AND THE SANTA MARIA, GARY DEANES TOOK ONE OF HIS PAPER PLATES AND FLUNG IT LIKE A FRISBEE. HE SAID THAT ONE WAS COLUMBUS. WE THOUGHT MRS. BROGAN'S HEAD WAS GONNA BLOW OFF, LIKE A VOLCANO IN A MOVIE.

FACE TURNING RED

VOICE LIKE THE EXORCIST

A PAPER PLATE IS NOT A TOY!!!

SPIT COMING OUT

BULGING VEINS ON NECK

THE WHOLE CLASS HAD TO STOP EVERYTHING AND WRITE AN ESSAY CALLED "PAPER PLATES. WHY I SHOULD NOT THROW THEM": IN MINE I WROTE DOWN: "BECAUSE YOU COULD PUT SOMEONES EYE OUT, WASTE OF THE EARTH'S MOST VALUABLE NATURAL RESOURCES, AND NO CONSIDERATION FOR OTHERS." WHICH, AS FAR AS MRS. BROGAN IS CONCERNED, IS THE CORRECT ANSWER TO NEARLY ANY QUESTION.

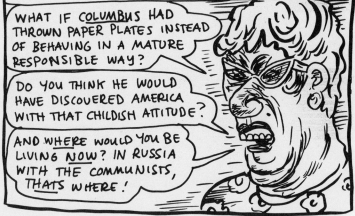

WHAT IF COLUMBUS HAD THROWN PAPER PLATES INSTEAD OF BEHAVING IN A MATURE RESPONSIBLE WAY?

DO YOU THINK HE WOULD HAVE DISCOVERED AMERICA WITH THAT CHILDISH ATTITUDE?

AND WHERE WOULD YOU BE LIVING NOW? IN RUSSIA WITH THE COMMUNISTS, THATS WHERE!

BAD FOR YOU

BY LYNDA ORSON WELLS BARRY ©1989

MRS. BROGAN TOLD THE LIGHT MONITOR TO TURN THE LIGHTS OFF THEN SHE SWITCHED ON THE OVERHEAD PROJECTOR AND SHOWED US ABOUT 40 PICTURES OF ROTTEN TEETH AND SAID THE SUBJECT OF THE DAY WAS POP.

A LOT OF YOU WILL END UP WITH TEETH EXACTLY LIKE THIS.

SHE SAID OF ALL POP, COKE WAS THE WORST AND IF YOU HUNG A HUNK OF MEAT IN A CAN OF COKE IT WOULD ROT RIGHT OFF THE STRING IN ONE DAY. SO THINK OF WHAT IT DOES TO YOUR STOMACH.

HOW MANY OF YOU LIKE THE THOUGHT OF BIG HOLES IN YOUR STOMACH LINING?

WHEN ARNOLD ARNESEN SHOWED UP THE NEXT DAY WITH A THERMOS FULL OF COKE AND A HOT DOG FLOATING IN IT MRS. BROGAN SAID "O.K., WE SHALL <u>SEE</u> WHAT HAPPENS" AND PUT THE THERMOS ON A TABLE BY ITSELF WITH AN INDEX CARD TAPED TO IT THAT SAID "EXPERIMENT"

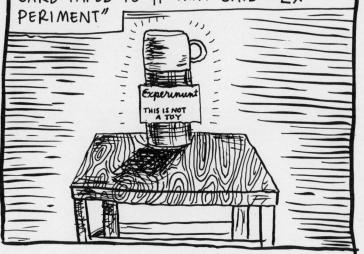

Experiment

THIS IS NOT A TOY

ALL DAY WE WONDERED ABOUT THE HOT DOG TRAPPED IN THE THERMOS WITH THE COKE. WHAT A HORRIBLE WAY TO GO.

AFTER 24 HOURS MRS. BROGAN TOOK US ALL OUT TO THE STORM DRAIN WHERE SHE WAS GOING TO POUR OUT THE COKE, AND SHE POURED IT AND THE HOT DOG FELL OUT IN PERFECT CONDITION.

FOR SOME REASON ALL OF US KNEW THIS WAS ABOUT THE SADDEST THING WE HAD EVER SEEN. ESPECIALLY MRS. BROGAN.

OTHER PLANETS

By LYNDA BARRY ©1987

EVERYONE IN OUR CLASS LOVED *the Solar System*. ESPECIALLY DRAWING IT. IT WAS SO PERFECTLY GORGEOUS.

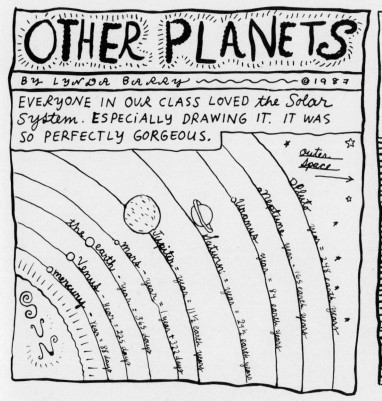

outer space →

ONE OF THE MAIN OBJECTS WAS TO GET THE NUMBER OF MOONS RIGHT FOR EACH PLANET. WE COULDN'T HELP FEELING GYPPED BY HOW EARTH ONLY GETS ONE. JUPITER GETS SOMETHING LIKE ELEVEN MOONS AND NO ONE EVEN USES THEM.

Darla Martles
May 3

Extra Credit Report

The Moons of the Planets

1. Mercury ○ (0) no moons
2. Venus ○ (0) no moons
3. Earth ○° (1) one moon
4. Mars ○°° (2) two moons
5. Jupiter ○ (11) eleven moons
6. Saturn (9) nine moons
7. Uranus ○ (4) four moons
8. Neptune ○° (1) one moon
9. Pluto ○ (0) no moons

Total of Moons = 28 moons

OF COURSE EVERYONE'S FAVORITE PLANET WAS SATURN BECAUSE IT TRULY LOOKED LIKE THE WORLD OF OUTER SPACE. IT WAS THE HARDEST PLANET TO DRAW ALTHOUGH A COUPLE PEOPLE WERE EXPERTS AT IT.

Darla Martles and Howard Grimes. The world's best drawers of Saturn

The Planet of SATURN

SATURN OUR 6TH PLANET

FOR THE ASSEMBLY OUR CLASS GOT TO ACT OUT THE SOLAR SYSTEM FOR THE REST OF THE SCHOOL. ONE GIRL CRIED BECAUSE ALL SHE GOT TO BE WAS A DISTANT STAR AND TWO BOYS GOT INTO A FIGHT OVER WHO GOT TO BE SATURN AND ONE GOT A BLOODY NOSE.

HEADS DOWN, CLASS. I'M ASHAMED OF YOUR BEHAVIOR THIS AFTER-NOON.

IF OUR SOLAR SYSTEM BEHAVED THE WAY YOU DID TODAY WE'D ALL BE IN BIG TROUBLE.

PHYSICAL EDUCATION

BY LYNDA ADORNMENT BARRY ©1987

IT WAS A BEAUTIFUL DAY IN MAY AND WHEN THE TWO A.V. GUYS BROUGHT THE RECORD PLAYER INTO OUR CLASS EVERYBODY KNEW THAT FOR P.E. MRS. BROGAN HAD SQUARE DANCING ON HER MIND.

CLASS, I HAVE A VERY SPECIAL SURPRISE FOR YOU TODAY AND IT INVOLVES, OUR NATIONS HERITAGE.

THERE WAS A CERTAIN MYSTERY ABOUT SQUARE DANCING THAT MADE OUR WHOLE CLASS ACT UP. MAYBE IT HAD SOMETHING TO DO WITH DANCING OUTSIDE TO THE EXCITED WIGGLING SOUNDS OF THE SONG "TURKEY IN THE STRAW." IT WAS A SITUATION THAT MADE YOUR PANTS ITCH.

READY?

I CAN'T START THE MUSIC UNTIL I SEE 32 GOOD CITIZENS.

CLASS?

WE CAN ALWAYS GO BACK INSIDE AND PUT OUR HEADS DOWN FOR 45 MINUTES...

THE SECOND MRS. BROGAN PUT ON THE MUSIC, THE THING TO DO WAS START ACTING LIKE A BEATNIK TO IT. YOU SORT OF CLOSED YOUR EYES AND SNAPPED YOUR FINGERS REALLY CLOSE TO YOUR FACE AND SAID BEATNIK MOTTOS. THAT WOULD ALWAYS MAKE US DIE LAUGHING.

DIG THAT CRAZY BEAT

GO MAN GO

THAT'S AWAY OUT

I DIG ON IT BABY

YEAH

COOL MAN COOL

MRS. BROGAN NEVER YELLED AT US FOR DOING IT EITHER BECAUSE IT SEEMS LIKE THAT SONG TURKEY IN THE STRAW JUST AUTOMATICALLY PUTS EVERYONE IN A GOOD MOOD.

OH IF ONLY MR. BROGAN WERE STILL WITH US CLASS! MY HUSBAND JUST LOVED TO DANCE TO THIS!

TUR-KEY IN THE HAAAY

SNAP SNAP

HOW things TURN out

by Lynda Barry © 86

"O.K. CHILDREN! LINE UP! WHO WANTS TO BE DOOR MONITOR TODAY?"

IN SCHOOL, OF COURSE, THERE WERE THE QUEEN GIRLS AND THEN THERE WERE THE REST AND AT THE BOTTOM OF THE REST WERE THE ONES, WHATEVER YOU WANT TO CALL THEM, THE ONES YOU WOULD BE ASHAMED TO HAVE TO TOUCH.

WE PRETTY MUCH KNEW WHO WE WERE BY SECOND GRADE BUT IT TOOK US UNTIL FOURTH TO REALIZE OUR POSITIONS WERE FIXED. OCCASIONALLY SOMEONE COULD GET LOWERED FOR, SAY, WETTING THEIR PANTS AT A FIELD TRIP BUT IT WAS ALMOST IMPOSSIBLE TO MOVE UP. THE ONLY GIRLS WHO EVEN TRIED WERE THE VERY BOTTOM ONES, FOR THIS WAS ABOUT THEIR ONLY ACTIVITY.

top

"ANGELA! YOU EITHER BE DEENA'S PARTNER OR YOU CAN GO TO THE OFFICE!"

"I'LL GO TO THE OFFICE."

bottom

EVEN IF YOU CHANGED SCHOOLS IT DIDN'T CHANGE. YOU WERE ALWAYS IN THE SAME PLACE. MONEY ONLY MATTERED KINDA. IF YOU WERE REALLY RICH YOU COULD NEVER BE AT THE VERY BOTTOM BECAUSE TOO MANY KIDS WOULD STILL WANT TO PLAY WITH YOUR STUFF. IF YOU WERE REALLY POOR YOU COULD NEVER BE ON TOP BECAUSE IT WAS JUST TOO EMBARASSING.

I CAN'T COME OVER BECAUSE MY MOM SAYS I'M NOT ALLOWED TO WALK AT WHERE YOU GUYSES LIVE.

IT HAD NOTHING TO DO WITH HOW SMART YOU WERE. AND EVEN IF YOU WEREN'T THAT CUTE, IF YOU WERE A QUEEN, PEOPLE WOULD COPY YOU. IT DIDN'T MATTER IF YOU WERE TEACHER'S PET OR NOT. IT WAS JUST SOMETHING DECIDED BETWEEN US, EVEN THOUGH IT WASN'T US WHO DECIDED IT. IT WAS SOMETHING WE ALL KNEW ABOUT. IT WAS OUR MAIN RULE OF LIFE.

ANGELA! AM I GOING TO HAVE TO SEND YOU TO THE OFFICE **AGAIN**?

SAY IT NOW!

IT'S O.K. MISS LEE, I GOT A BAD STOMACHACHE SO I'LL JUST GO TO THE NURSES AND ANGELA WON'T HAVE TO HOLD MY HAND.

BEAN PLANTS

By LYNDA BARRY ©1987

ALL YOU NEED FOR LEARNING ABOUT THE PLANT KINGDOM IS: YOUR MILK CARTON THAT YOU SAVED FROM LUNCH, SOME DIRT, SOME WATER, SOME BEANS, SOME SARAN WRAP, SOME RUBBER BANDS AND YOUR TEACHER MRS. BROGAN YELLING AT YOU TO NOT GOOF UP IN ANY WAY.

COVER IT WITH THE SARAN WRAP TO KEEP IT WARM AND THE WONDER OF EVAPORATION

MILK

REMEMBER. THESE ARE THE EARTH'S NATURAL RESOURCES SO BE RESPONSIBLE CITIZENS AND DON'T MAKE A MESS. MR. BEAN IS DEPENDING ON YOU TODAY FOR A GOOD HOME.

YOU WILL HAVE A GREAT FEELING WHEN YOUR BEAN STARTS TO GROW. YOU WILL HAVE TO SHARPEN YOUR PENCIL A LOT JUST FOR AN EXCUSE TO PASS BY IT.

ARNA! THE PENCIL SHARPENER IS NOT A TOY.

MILK MILK MILK MILK
MILK MILK MILK M

SOMEONE GOT THE IDEA TO NAME THEIR BEAN PLANT AND PRETTY SOON EVERY-ONE DID IT.

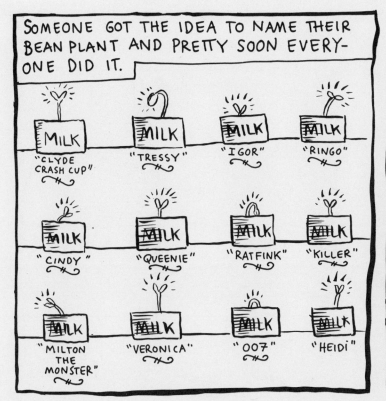

"CLYDE CRASH CUP"

"TRESSY"

"IGOR"

"RINGO"

"CINDY"

"QUEENIE"

"RATFINK"

"KILLER"

"MILTON THE MONSTER"

"VERONICA"

"007"

"HEIDI"

FINALLY ON THE LAST DAY OF SCHOOL YOU GET TO TAKE YOUR BEAN PLANT HOME. AFTER SHE GAVE US ALL OUR PLANTS, MRS. BROGAN STOOD AT THE FRONT OF THE ROOM TO SAY GOOD BYE. SHE TOLD US WE WERE A LOVELY CLASS AND SHE WILL MISS US VERY MUCH. AND SHE STARTED TO CRY WHEN SHE TOLD US TO BE SURE TO REMEMBER TO WATER OUR BEANS.

RRRIINNGGGGG

Ss Tt Qq Vv Ww Xx Yy Zz

GIRLSCOUTS

BY LYNDA "SKUNK CABBAGE" BARRY · FOR HOLLY ©1986

OUR GIRLSCOUT LEADER WAS A CHAIN SMO-KING, ENORMOUSLY FAT WOMAN WITH DYED HAIR NAMED MRS. BONA. SHE HAD A SPOILED DAUGHTER NAMED BRENDA BONA AND THERE WAS NO DAD.

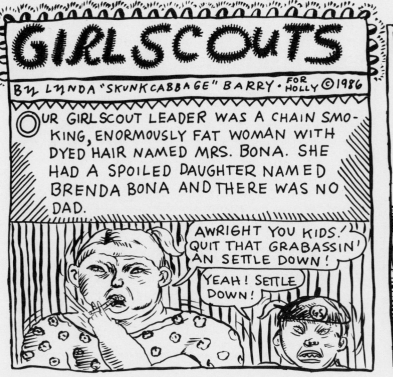

AWRIGHT YOU KIDS! QUIT THAT GRABASSIN' AN SETTLE DOWN!

YEAH! SETTLE DOWN!

BEFORE OUR FIRST CAMPOUT MRS. BONA SAID WE ALL HAD TO PICK A NICK-NAME. SHE SAID HERS WAS GOING TO BE "BABY-DOLL". WE TRIED NOT TO LAUGH. I PICKED "SKUNK CABBAGE" FOR ME AND MY FRIEND PICKED "AGENT 99".

BRENDA BONA PICKED "ANGEL HAIR" SO NATURALLY WE CALLED HER "BUTT HAIR" BUT NOT IN FRONT OF MRS. BONA.

MA! THE OTHER GIRLS ARE MAKIN' FUNNA ME AGAIN! THEIR CALLIN' ME, UH— "REAR-END HAIR" STEADA MY REAL NICK NAME!

HAVE A DOUGHNUT HONEY.

I'LL TAKE CARE OF IT.

WE WERE ASSIGNED TO BRING FOOD FOR THE CAMPOUT AND ALMOST EVERYONE WAS SUPPOSED TO BRING MEAT. I HAD TO BRING 15 PORK CHOPS. MY FRIEND HAD TO BRING 8 PACKAGES OF BACON. WE HELPED MRS. BONA LOAD IT INTO HER FREEZER IN THE BASEMENT THAT HAD A PADLOCK ON IT AND WE NEVER SAW IT AGAIN. ON THE CAMPOUT ALL WE ATE WAS SHREDDED WHEAT, MACARONI AND CHEESE, AND POCKET STEW. SOME GIRLS CRIED.

"Pocket Stew" "COOKED ON A CAMPFIRE"

BURNT TIN FOIL

BURNT POTATOES AND CARROTS THAT ARE STILL HARD

BURNT WADS OF NASTY HAMBURGER RAW INSIDE

GIRLS → CRYING

BURNT ↓ ONIONS

EVEN THOUGH THE FOOD WAS BAD AND IT WAS FREEZING COLD, MRS. BONA SAT IN HER CAR THE WHOLE TIME WITH THE ENGINE GOING, SO WE COULD DO WHAT WE WANTED. MY FRIEND AND I HAD THE IDEA OF MAKING SOME CIGARETTES OUT OF LEAVES AND TOILET PAPER AND BURNED OUR EYEBROWS OFF.

OOOH! I'M TELLIN' MY MOM! YOU'RE IN FOR IT NOW! YOU'RE GONNA GET CREAMED FOR THIS! I AM THE QUEEN OF THE ENTIRE WORLD!

AGUGHH!

WOOSH

AFTER THE CAMPOUT SOME GIRLS HAD TO DROP OUT OF GIRLSCOUTS WHEN THEIR PARENTS FOUND OUT ABOUT THE MEAT. THAT WAS SAD FOR US. THE OTHER PROBLEM WAS BADGE MONEY. EVERY BODY HAD TO BRING 35¢ FOR EACH BADGE THEY EARNED AND MRS. BONA GAVE US BADGES LIKE CRAZY. WE BROUGHT THE MONEY AND SHE SAID SHE TURNED IT IN BUT THE BADGES NEVER CAME.

ONE MORE WORD ABOUT THEM BADGES AND YOU'VE HAD IT, YOU UNDERSTAND ME? I TOLD YOU THEY HAVE TO BE SENT ALL THE WAY FROM FRANCE AND IT TAKES A LONG TIME. NOW LETS SING KUM-BY-YUH.

THE LAST TIME WE SAW MRS. BONA WAS THE FINAL TIME TO TURN IN YOUR GIRLSCOUT COOKIE MONEY. THE NEXT WEEK WHEN WE CAME FOR OUR MEETING HER HOUSE WAS JUST STANDING THERE, ALL EMPTY WITH NO ONE IN IT.
LATER WE HAD A DIFFERENT LEADER BUT IT WAS NEVER AS GOOD AGAIN.

TROOP, I FEEL IT WOULD BE BETTER FOR ALL OF US TO FORGET MRS. BONA AND START FRESH IN THIS EXCITING WORLD OF GIRL SCOUTING....
SO LET'S SING KUM-BI-YA. WHO WOULD LIKE TO LEAD?

TALENT SHOW

By LYNDA BUDDY GUY BARRY © 1986 seattle

SOMETIMES LIKE ON A SUNDAY AND YOU'RE STUCK AT YOUR COUSINS AND THERE AIN'T ONE DECENT THING TO DO BESIDES WATCHING DUMB STUPID "ROMAN THEATER" (— ONE MILLION BLACK AND WHITE MOVIES ABOUT GLADIATORS —) WELL WHY NOT HAVE A TALENT SHOW OR SOMETHING?

TESTING TESTING LADIES AND GENTLEMEN FOR NOW LET ME INTRODUCE THE GREAT MARLYS GONNA DO SOME TUMBLEING FOR YOU NOW. LET'S HEAR IT FOR MARLYS!

LIKE YOU CAN DO AN ACTING OF YOUR FAVORITE MOVIE.

OR YOU CAN DO SOME INCREDIBLE THING TO MAKE PEOPLE AMAZED BY YOU.

I VANT TO SUCK YOUR BLOOD. BETTER WATCH OUT BECAUSE I VANT TO SUCK YOUR BLOOD!

I WILL NOW EAT THE SIX RAW HOT DOGS WITHOUT STOPPING 'TIL THEY ARE GONE.

THE MUSIC TO IT WILL BE "REVOLUTION" BY THE BEATLES.

BELIEVE IT OR NOT

BY LYNDA BARRY ©1987

OUR FAVORITE BOOK OF ALL TIME WAS BY RIPLEY CALLED RIPLEY'S BELIEVE IT OR NOT. WE ENJOYED A LOT OF THE PICTURES AND STORIES. IN OUR OPINION THAT'S THE BOOK THEY SHOULD TEACH READING WITH.

(PALL MALL)

FRANK BROWN WOUNDED SOLDIER CAN SMOKE A CIGARETTE THRU A HOLE IN HIS FOREHEAD.

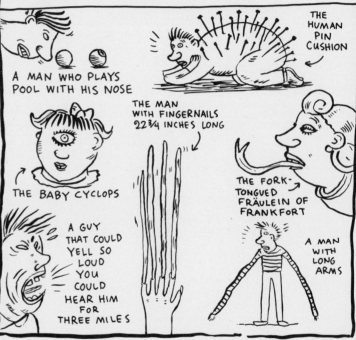

IN THIS BOOK YOU CAN LEARN ABOUT A LOT OF INTERESTING PEOPLE.

A MAN WHO PLAYS POOL WITH HIS NOSE

THE HUMAN PIN CUSHION

THE MAN WITH FINGERNAILS 22¾ INCHES LONG

THE BABY CYCLOPS

THE FORK-TONGUED FRÄULEIN OF FRANKFORT

A GUY THAT COULD YELL SO LOUD YOU COULD HEAR HIM FOR THREE MILES

A MAN WITH LONG ARMS

ALSO THERE WERE MANY INTERESTING ANIMALS TO EXPLORE.

A CHICKEN WHO LAID TWO SQUARE EGGS

A FISH THAT CAN CLIMB TREES

THE MAN EATING CLAM

A BIRD CALLED "THE LAUGHING JACK ASS"

THE PEG-LEG COW

A TOAD THAT HOPPED 75 MILES IN FIVE DAYS

THE WONDER WEENIE
A 885 POUND HOT DOG THAT WAS HALF A MILE LONG

ALL OF US DREAMED OF SOMEDAY BEING IN THAT BOOK.

ARNOLD: JUMPED OFF THE PORCH 37 TIMES WITHOUT STOPPING. —COULD HAVE DONE MORE BUT HIS MOM MADE HIM QUIT.

FOUND: A PEANUT WITH THREE THINGS IN IT.

FOUND: TWO M&Ms STUCK TOGETHER (GREEN)

ARNA: COULD FIT A LOT OF MARBLES IN HER MOUTH

CHEWED: 1 PIECE OF GUM, 11 DAYS STILL GOOD

MADE: RUBBER BAND CHAIN ONE BLOCK LONG

ALL THE LIVE LONG DAY

FREDDIE: CAUGHT 19 BEES IN ONE JAR

MARLYS: SANG "CAMP TOWN RACES" 100 TIMES IN A ROW ON A LONG CAR TRIP BUT HAD TO HUM THE LAST 72 TIMES OR HER MOM SAID SHE'D GET IT.

D.O.G. P.A.R.T.Y.

BY LYNDA THE ENTHRALLER BARRY © 1986

DICKIE HINES SAID HIS DOG JIGS'S BUTT LOOKED EXACTLY LIKE A PENNY AND HE SAID TAKE A LOOK IF YOU DON'T BELIEVE IT AND MY BROTHER HELD A PENNY AND I HELD JIGS AND MRS. HINES WALKED IN AS USUAL AND CREAMED DICKIE WHO WASN'T DOING NOTHING. CHILDREN ARE JUST NATURALLY CURIOUS.

MY GOTT IN HIMMEL!! WHAT ARE YOU DOING TO THAT DOG!!

ANOTHER TRICK JIGS COULD DO WAS WHEN DICKIE GOT A SLICE OF BALONEY AND SAT IN THEIR NEW CHAIR THEY HAD WHICH COULD SPIN AROUND. HE WOULD HANG ON TO JIGS'S COLLAR AND HOLD THE BALONEY RIGHT BY JIGS'S FACE AND JIGS WOULD CHASE THAT LUNCHMEAT AND TWIRL DICKIE IN THE CHAIR ABOUT A THOUSAND TIMES UNTIL ONCE WHEN THE CHAIR BROKE. IN OUR OPINION JIGS WAS A TERRIFIC DOG.

THE ONLY PROBLEM WITH JIGS WAS HE WOULD CHASE CARS AND TRY TO BITE THE TIRES BECAUSE HE DID NOT HAVE NO SAFETY HABITS. MR. HENDERSON WHO WATCHED EVERYTHING FROM HIS PORCH SAID THE ONLY THING THAT WOULD TEACH THAT DOG A LESSON WAS BY SHOOTING HIM. DICKIE SAID MR. HENDERSON COULD LEARN A LESSON THE SAME WAY.

ONE BORING DAY DICKIE FIGURED OUT TO HAVE A PARTY FOR JIGS AND IN HONOR OF IT WE WERE GOING TO HAVE EVERY DOG IN THE NEIGHBORHOOD COME OVER. WE HAD TO LIBERATE ALL THE DOGS WE KNEW WHO WERE TIED UP OR FENCED IN. OUR MOTTO WAS "FREE ALL THE DOGS." WE WILL NEVER DO THAT AGAIN.

23rd STREET WAS OUR LIMIT BECAUSE THERE WERE ALWAYS TEN MILLION CARS GOING ON IT GOING WAY TOO FAST. NO NORMAL MOM WOULD TELL THEIR KID GO AHEAD AND CROSS IT. IT WAS SCARY EVEN TO US, SORT OF. WELL ALL OF A SUDDEN NEE NEE RUNS OUT INTO THE STREET, NO ONE EVEN KNOWS WHY AND THE CAR CAN'T STOP AND SUDDENLY WE ARE ALL RUNNING HOME THINKING IF WE CAN GO FAST ENOUGH, IT DIDN'T REALLY HAPPEN.

WE HEARD THE SIRENS OF THE AMBULANCE AND LIKE USUAL EVERY MOM THAT WAS HOME STEPPED OUT ON THE PORCH WIPING THEIR HANDS ON THEIR DRESS AND LOOKING QUICK TO MAKE SURE IT WASN'T THEIR CHILD THAT AMBULANCE IS COMING FOR. WHEN NEE-NEE'S MAMA CAME OUT WELL WE JUST STOOD THERE NORMAL LIKE WE DIDN'T KNOW NOTHING.

CATALOG

PART ONE

LYNDA "EARL AVENUE" BARRY © 1987

THE FIRST TIME I EVER GOT ANYTHING FROM THE CATALOG, IT WAS A BABY TINY TEARS. BABY TINY TEARS CAME WITH A WHOLE WAD OF ACCESSORIES WHICH IS THE BEST PART OF ANY DOLL.

MINIATURE WASHCLOTH

"MOLDED" HAIR

DIAPER

SCARY MOUTH

PACIFIER

LITTLE SPONGE

TINY BAR OF SOAP

IVORY

BOTTLE

Tiny Tears

DRESS

BONNET

MIDGET KLEENEXS

TINY TEARS TISSUE

BOOTIES THAT WON'T STAY ON

SHRIMPY BUBBLE PIPE

SHE HAD THIS KIND OF MOUTH WITH A TINY HOLE IN IT THAT YOU COULD STICK THE END OF A PENCIL IN AND MAKE IT LOOK LIKE SHE WAS SMOKING. THE BAD THING WAS IF YOU TRIED TO USE A PEN AND YOU MISSED.
ONCE YOU GET BLUE BALL POINT INK ON A DOLL HEAD, THATS IT. IT'S WRECKED FOR LIFE.

CIGARS? CIGARETTES? TIPPARILLOS?

UH-OH.

THE OTHER THING WAS THAT SHE WOULD "WET" OUT OF HER SHOULDERS, HER NECK, AND HER EYEBALLS IF YOU ACCIDENTLY HUNG HER UPSIDE DOWN AFTER YOU FED HER

OH NOT AGAIN!

YOU WERE SUPPOSED TO ONLY LET HER DRINK WATER BUT SOME OF US FELT SORRY FOR BABY TINY TEARS AND LET HER DRINK MILK. THIS WAS A BIG MISTAKE, ESPECIALLY IF IT WAS SUMMER AND YOU LET HER TAKE A NAP IN THE HOT SUN FOR ABOUT FIVE HOURS AFTERWARDS. I TELL YOU, YOU WILL NEVER PLAY WITH THAT DOLL AGAIN.

CATALOG

BY LYNDA BOUNCY SPRINGS BARRY © 1987

PART TWO: MARLYS PICKS

I TRIED TO WARN MARLYS THAT THEM RUBBER GLAMOR WIGS WEREN'T GOING TO BE NO GOOD. I MEAN ONE LOOK AT THE PICTURES IN THE CATALOG AND ANYBODY WOULD KNOW.

EXCLUSIVE MOLDED RUBBER GLAMOUR WIGS FOR YOUR YOUNG LITTLE MISS. SOPHISTICATED STYLES, WASHABLE, LIFE LIKE, EASY TO WEAR.
BLONDE, BRUNETTE, REDHEAD..........
3 PC SET $3.98

HER MOM SAID SHE COULD ORDER PRACTICALLY ANY TOY AND SHE PICKS THE <u>WIGS</u>. WHY NOT "MR. FREEZE" SO WE COULD MAKE SNO-KONES? OR A DOLL HOUSE 5 ROOMS COMPLETELY FURNISHED?

YOU COULD SET UP YOUR OWN SNOKONE STAND AND MAKE 'BOUT A MILLION BUCKS!

I CAN'T HEAR YOU
I CAN'T HEAR YOU
I CAN'T HEAR YOU
I CAN'T HEAR YOU

YOU GET THAT DOLL HOUSE AND ALL THE GIRLS WHO HATE US WILL WANT TO COME OVER AND WE'LL BE POPULAR!

WHEN THE WIGS FINALLY CAME THEY WERE ABOUT FIVE HUNDRED TIMES WORSE THAN I EVER COULD HAVE IMAGINED. MARLYS STARTED CRYING AND FOR ONCE I DIDN'T BLAME HER. THEY LOOKED LIKE A BATHING CAP WITH WITH A BAD INFECTION. LIKE KAL-TIKI THE IMMORTAL MONSTER. LIKE OLD GUM IN THE DIRT.

CAN YOU EVEN BELIEVE IT?!

THE MINUTE MY BROTHER SAW THEM THOUGH, HE FIGURED OUT A WHOLE GAME WITH THEM BASED ON A MOVIE WE ALL LOVED CALLED "DIE MONSTER DIE" WHERE YOUR HEAD GETS TOTALLY DEFORMED. AND THOSE SEARS WIGS WERE ABOUT THE BEST DEFORMED THINGS WE EVER SAW. IT TURNED OUT TO BE THE FAVORITE GAME OF OUR LIFE.

K'MON MARLYS, YOU ALWAYS GET TO BE BORIS KARLOFF.

NO FAIR.

WHO'S WIGS ARE THEY, HUH? I'M BORIS KARLOFF FOR LIFE.

DANG.

K'MON MARLYS!

CATALOG

BY LYNDA BEEFARONI BARRY © 1987

PART THREE: ARMY MEN

MY BROTHER HAD $7.00 FROM COMBINATION CHRISTMAS AND BIRTHDAY MONEY SO HE HAD MOM ORDER HIM **TWO** SETS (75 PIECES EACH) OF "THE ARMY TRAINING CAMP." I SAID "WHY YOU GOTTA GET TWO OF THE SAME THING?" HE LOOK AT ME LIKE I WAS A TOTAL IDIOT.

"THIS IS SARGENT ARNOLD, OVER."

"NO. HOLD ON. THIS IS MAJOR ARNOLD, OVER."

"NO. WAIT A SEC... THIS IS ARNOLD, GREEN BERET, OVER."

WHEN THEY FINALLY CAME HE TOOK ABOUT TWO HOURS TO FIX IT ALL IN A LONG ROW OUT ON THE FRONT SIDE WALK.

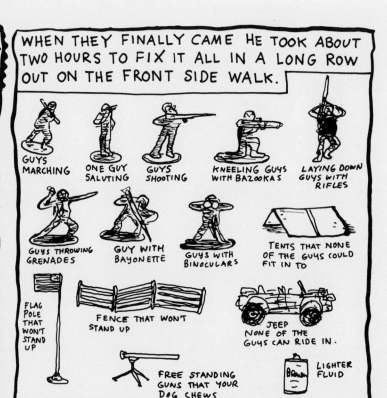

GUYS MARCHING

ONE GUY SALUTING

GUYS SHOOTING

KNEELING GUYS WITH BAZOOKAS

LAYING DOWN GUYS WITH RIFLES

GUYS THROWING GRENADES

GUY WITH BAYONETTE

GUYS WITH BINOCULARS

TENTS THAT NONE OF THE GUYS COULD FIT IN TO

FLAG POLE THAT WON'T STAND UP

FENCE THAT WON'T STAND UP

JEEP NONE OF THE GUYS CAN RIDE IN.

FREE STANDING GUNS THAT YOUR DOG CHEWS

LIGHTER FLUID

THE NEXT DAY HE SETS UP A WHOLE WAR OUT IN THE GARDEN. HE MADE A REALISTIC LAKE FROM A MIRROR PART BURIED IN THE DIRT. HE MADE A RIVER FROM THE GARDEN HOSE. HE MADE PARACHUTERS OUT OF HANKERCHIEFS. HE HAD THE WHOLE THING SET UP PERFECTLY, THEN HE GOT A BOWL OF CEREAL AND ATE IT OUT ON THE GRASS AND JUST LOOKED AT IT ALL. THEN HE TOOK HIS BOWL IN THE HOUSE, CAME OUT AND BLEW THE WHOLE THING UP WITH DIRT BOMBS.

AAGGGH!
BLAM-BLAM-BLAM!
KA-BLOOEY!
No! No! NOOOOO!
RATA-TAT-TAT-TAT-TAT-TAT
I'LL GET YOU YOU DIRTY LITTLE
BLASH!
BLAM!
HELP! HAVE MERCY!
BLAM!
DUCK!
KER-PLUNK!
BLAMMO!

ON THE THIRD DAY I SMELL A TERRIBLE BURNING SMELL AND I CAN HEAR MY BROTHER UNDER THE PORCH WITH HIS MEN. I SNEAK AROUND AND SEE HIM WITH THE LIGHTER FLUID, MATCHES AND HE HOLDS UP THIS ONE GUY HE JUST LIT ON FIRE AND PART OF IT MELTS ON MY BROTHERS HAND AND HE YELLS AND HE STILL HAS THE SCAR FROM THAT TOO.

YOUCH!
HEY MAN NO FAIR!
OW-OW OW-O-W OOOW!
CHHHHHH!

CATALOG

By LYNDA SPRAY 'N' WASH BARRY © 1987

Part Four: MISC.

—HERE ARE SOME TOYS OUR MOM REFUSED TO EVER BUY US, AND WHY.

SPECIAL SPOONS

ICE GOES IN HEAD

CRANK IT

OUT COMES SHAVED ICE TO MAKE SNO-KONES

Mr. Frosty Freeze

MOM: "A LADY I WORK WITH GOT THAT FOR HER KIDS AND THEY ENDED UP THROWING UP FOR TWO DAYS."

BALLERINA WATCH — HER LEGS TELL THE TIME"

MOM: YOUR COUSIN HAD ONE, AND THOSE LEGS FELL OFF IN LESS THAN A WEEK."

THE SPARKLING ELECTRIC BURP GUN. — shoots sparks

MOM: "EVERYTIME I SMELL ONE OF THOSE THINGS, I THINK THE T.V. IS BURNING. I DON'T NEED THE HEART ACHE. BESIDES, IT TORMENTS THE DOG."

THE LITTLE RED SCOOTER

MOM: "YOUR COUSIN FREDDIE WENT OVER THE ROCKERY AND BROKE HIS COLLARBONE RIDING ONE OF THOSE."

MODEL FARM SET WITH STEEL BARN AND ONE PLASTIC TREE AND ABOUT 25 ANIMALS

MOM: "THAT'S HOW COME ONE OF NORMA'S KIDS ENDED UP IN THE HOSPITAL. HE WAS SUCKING ON ONE OF THOSE PLASTIC CHICKENS AND HIS BROTHER HIT HIM IN THE BACK AND THAT CHICKEN LODGED IN HIS WINDPIPE. I TELL YOU, IT'S A WONDER HE SURVIVED."

RUBBER TIPPED DART GUN SET.

MOM: "OH NO. I KNOW ALL ABOUT THOSE THINGS. YOU KIDS SUCK ON THE ENDS OF THOSE DARTS TO MAKE THEM STICK BETTER THEN THERE ARE SPIT RINGS ALL OVER THE WINDOWS AND T.V. SCREEN. ALL OVER THE WALLS. FORGET IT. BESIDES I READ IN THE PAPER WHERE A BOY PUT HIS EYE OUT WITH A GUN LIKE THAT"

PACESETTER "CONVERTABLE" WITH BALL BEARING PEDAL DRIVE

MOM: "THOSE THINGS ARE GREAT UNTIL YOU GO DOWN A STEEP HILL. THEN THOSE PEDALS WILL RIP YOUR LEGS OFF"

"MUSICAL JACK IN THE BOX"

PLAYS "POP GOES THE WEASEL"

MOM: I'M TELLING YOU, ONCE I GET THAT SONG IN MY HEAD I CAN'T GET IT OUT AND I JUST HEAR IT FAS- TER AND FASTER UNTIL I FEEL LIKE I'M IN AN INSANE ASYLUM. THAT TOY SHOULD BE AGAINST THE LAW. AND DON'T EVER LET ME CATCH YOU SINGING IT."

THE CARNIVAL

By LYNDA SWANG THANG BARRY © 1986

WE DECIDED TO HAVE A CARNIVAL SHOW AND WE DECIDED TO HAVE IT ON A DAY WHEN NO ONE'S PARENTS WOULD BE ANYWHERE EXCEPT AT WORK. OUR MAIN ATTRACTION WAS GOING TO BE: "THINGS LIGHTED ON FIRE". OUR MAIN PROBLEM WAS GOING TO BE: "MARLYS TELLING".

YOU THINK YOU'RE SO BIG.

YOU'RE NOT THE BOSS OF US MARLYS.

I'M GONNA WRITE DOWN EVERYTHING YOU DO.

WHY DON'T YOU GO BACK INSIDE AND WATCH YOURSELF IN THE MIRROR SOME MORE?

THEN I'M GOING TO HAVE YOU PUT IN JAIL.

LIGTER FLUID

MY SISTER AND DEENA WERE GOING TO DO A SPECIAL TUMBLING SHOW TO THE SONG "LOVE IS BLUE". TO GET THE MUSIC THEY HAD TO PUT IT ON FULL BLAST AND PUSH THE RECORD PLAYER OVER BY THE WINDOW. MARLYS WAS GOING TO TELL ON THEM FOR THAT TOO.

CAN YOU HEAR IT GOOD?!

LOUDER!

IT CAN'T GO NO LOUDER!

PUSH IT MORE BY THE WINDOW!

THERES NO MORE PLUG!

YOUR MOM SAID NEVER TOUCH HER RECORD PLAYER BUT YOU HAD TO DO IT, DIDN'T YOU?

I'M WRITING YOU A TICKET.

MARLYS WAS MAKING A HARD TIME FOR EVERYBODY TO THINK UP THINGS TO DO BECAUSE NO MATTER WHAT YOU THOUGHT OF, SHE SAID SHE'D TELL ON YOU FOR IT. AND SHE <u>WOULD</u> TOO. FINALLY SOMEONE HAD THE GENIUS TO ASK MARLYS TO BE THE STAR OF THE SHOW.

YEAH MARLYS! YOU CAN BE THE MAIN QUEEN!

YOU CAN WEAR MY MAMA'S HIGH HEELS!

COME ON MARLYS!

YOU CAN HOLD THE MATCHES!

YOU CAN ANNOUNCE EVERYBODY!

WE'LL EVEN LISTEN TO YOU SINGING!

YEAH! COME ON MARLYS!

FOR ABOUT ONE SECOND MARLYS STOOD THERE LOOKING AT US LIKE SHE NEVER EVEN MET US BEFORE. THEN SHE WENT OUT OF HER MIND AND YELLED "I HATE YOU I HATE YOU ALL" ABOUT 600 TIMES UNTIL SHE WAS PRACTICALLY DROOLING. IT SCARED US AND DEENA AND MY SISTER STARTED CRYING ALONG WITH MARLYS WHO WOULDN'T EVEN LET US COME NEAR HER. AFTER THAT WE REALIZED IT WAS A LOT BETTER FOR MARLYS IF YOU JUST KEPT TREATING HER LIKE YOU HATED HER GUTS.

BATON

BY LYNDA SHILLY SHALLY BARRY © 1987

UP AT THE SCHOOL, ON SATURDAY MORNINGS IN THE SUMMER WAS <u>BATON LESSONS</u> TAUGHT BY TWO GLAMOUROUS TEEN AGERS, <u>LILA</u> AND <u>BARB</u>, OUR PERFECT IDOLS, THE MOST PERFECT GIRLS IN THE WORLD, OUR TOTAL HEROS.

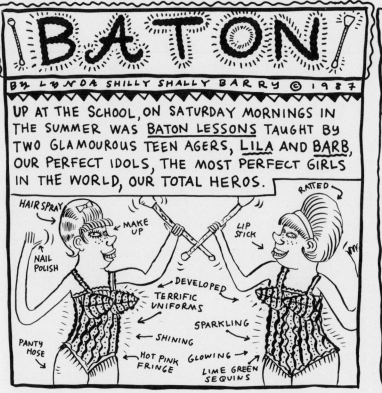

TO BE IN THE CLASS, YOU HAD TO GET YOUR BATON FROM THE PAY 'N' SAVE AT THE BOTTOM OF THE HILL, WHERE THEY HAD BEEN ESPECIALLY ORDERED. FROM THE SECOND YOU GOT IT, YOU FELT TOTALLY DIFFERENT.

THERE WAS SOMETHING ABOUT EVEN HOLDING A BATON THAT COULD GIVE YOU THE MYSTERIOUS EXCITED FEELING. ALMOST LIKE IF YOU JUST HELD IT LONG ENOUGH YOU WOULD AUTOMATICALLY GROW INTO A GORGEOUS BEAUTY PAGENT WINNER, FULLY DEVELOPED.

IN THE MEAN TIME, WHAT YOU DID WITH IT, WAS THROW IT UP IN THE AIR AS HIGH AS YOU COULD, TWIRL AROUND, THEN TRY NOT TO MOVE WHEN IT LANDED ON YOU. WE GOT HIT ABOUT A MILLION TIMES BUT IN OUR OPINION IT WAS WORTH IT.

BIKES

BY LYNDA HIPPY-MAN BARRY © 1 9 8 7

THIS ONLY A STORY ABOUT OUR BIKES. LIKE MY FIRST ONE, ASSEMBLY NOT INCLUDED, WITH TRAINING WHEELS, FROM SEARS. IF YOU HAVE TRAINING WHEELS EVERYONE WILL YELL "BABY" AT YOU, SO BETTER GO AHEAD AND TAKE THEM OFF AND JUST MAKE SURE YOU'RE BY SOME BUSHES WHEN YOU START TO WIPE OUT.

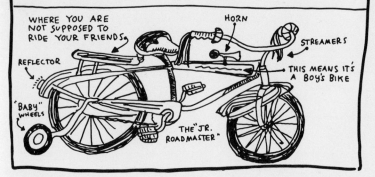

WHERE YOU ARE NOT SUPPOSED TO RIDE YOUR FRIENDS

HORN

STREAMERS

REFLECTOR

THIS MEANS IT'S A BOY'S BIKE

"BABY" WHEELS

THE "JR. ROADMASTER"

THE NEXT BIKE, ME AND MY BROTHER HAD TO SHARE. A SEARS STING RAY "SPYDER" ALL GOLD WITH BUTTERFLY HANDLE BARS, A LEOPARD SKIN BANANA SEAT AND A GIANT SISSY BAR. WE PUT TONY THE TIGER HANDLES ON IT AND ABOUT A HUNDRED CLOTHES PINS WITH PLAYING CARDS ON THE WHEELS TO MAKE IT SOUND LIKE A ACTUAL DRAGSTER. YOU COULD TELL IT WAS THE BEST BIKE IN THE WORLD JUST BY LOOKING AT IT.

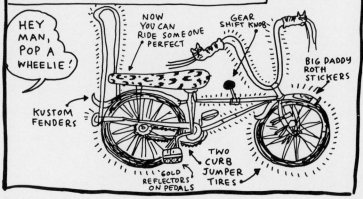

HEY MAN, POP A WHEELIE!

NOW YOU CAN RIDE SOMEONE PERFECT

GEAR SHIFT KNOB

BIG DADDY ROTH STICKERS

KUSTOM FENDERS

GOLD REFLECTORS ON PEDALS

TWO CURB JUMPER TIRES

OUR THING TO DO WAS GO UP THIS ONE HILL AFTER DARK WITH OUR BIKES AND TWO POP CANS WHICH YOU STEPPED ON SIDEWAYS REALLY HARD SO THEY MOLDED TO THE BACK OF YOUR SHOES. THEN EVERYBODY GETS IN A LINE AND WHEN THE GUY AT THE BOTTOM YELLS "NO CARS!" YOU <u>TAKE OFF</u> DRAGGING THOSE CANS ON THE <i>STREET</i> AND IT MAKES TERRIFIC SPARKS FLYING ALL OVER. WE CALLED THIS "THE TORCH-LIGHT PARADE."

TIMES!! MY CAN IS COMING OFF. YELL FOR HIM TO HANG ON A SEC.

OK?! NO CARS!!

OF COURSE SOMETIMES YOU JUST DON'T LISTEN TO ADVICE ON GOOD BIKE SAFETY ABOUT "DON'T RIDE YOUR FRIENDS DOWN THAT ONE PERFECT HILL THAT GOES TO THE A+P WITH NO BRAKES." THE ONLY LAW WE HAD ABOUT WIPING OUT WAS AFTER YOU WIPED OUT, NO MATTER HOW MUCH IT HURT, YOU HAD TO YELL "RUPTURE!" FIRST, WHICH WOULD USUALLY MAKE YOU START LAUGHING AT THE SAME TIME YOU WERE CRYING BECAUSE YOU'RE BLEEDING AND MAN LOOK HOW WRECKED-UP YOUR BIKE IS.

← BIKE UPSIDE DOWN WITH WHEEL STILL SPINNING

RUPTURE!

RUPTURE!

RUPTURE!

OW

DANG!

OLD RED
by LYNDA BARRY ©86

UP ON THE OTHER SIDE OF THE HILL, WHO THEY HAD WAS "BIG JUNIOR". OURS WAS "OLD RED", A NAKED MAN WHO HID IN THE BUSHES JUST WAITING FOR YOU TO COME UP THE 127 WOODEN STEPS THAT CUT THROUGH THE WOODS. HE WASN'T NO JOKE. HE WAS REAL.

HE CAME OUT ONCE BEHIND RHONDA'S TEEN-AGE SISTER AND KNOCKED HER TO THE GROUND AND YANKED ONE OF HER SHOES OFF AND RAN INTO THE WOODS WITH IT. RHONDA SAYS THATS WHY EDNA HANGS OUT WITH THE HOODLIMS UP AT THE SCHOOL AND SNIFFS GLUE OFF OF MEN'S SOCKS IN A BAG. BECAUSE SHE'S STILL UPSET ABOUT OLD RED.

OLD RE-ED!

YOO HOO!

QUIT!

SHOOT. I AINTA FRAID OF NO OLD UGLY NAKED MAN. HE COME OUT, I JUST THROW ME A ROCK AND KNOCK HIS DINGER OFF.

SURE

OK. I'LL PROVE IT IF YA DON'T BELIEVE ME.

HEY EDNA!

BUG OFF MAN!

HEY EDNA, TELL THESE TWO STUPID IDIOTS HOW COME YOU HADTA START SNIFFING GLUE

ONE DAY SHE GONNA GET TOO HIGH AN FALL OFF THIS MONKEY BAR AN BUST HER HEAD OPEN.

ONE GUY, LEONARD, SAID OLD RED WAS HIS FRIEND AND HE WENT OVER TO HIS HIDE-A-WAY ALL THE TIME AND SMOKED CIGARS WITH HIM. HE SAID OLD RED HAD A PILE OF SHOES TEN FEET HIGH AND COLLECTING SHOES WAS HIS MAIN HOBBY. WE ALL KNEW LEONARD WAS A TOTAL LIAR THOUGH.

IF YOU KNOW WHERE HE AT, WHY CAN'T YOU TAKE US THERE?

I GAVE HIM MY WORD OF HONOR THAT I WOULD NEVER TELL WHERE HE LIVES.

THEN BRING US ONE OF THEM CIGARS YOU SAY YOU ALWAYS SMOKIN'!

SOME NIGHTS WE WOULD SNEAK OUT AND MEET BY THE STEPS AND DARE EACH OTHER TO GO DOWN TO THE BOTTOM AND BACK UP ALONE. WHEN IT WAS MY TURN I JUST IMAGINED MY GUARDIAN ANGEL FLYING ABOVE, HOLDING A BIG STICK TO BASH OLD RED'S BRAINS OUT WITH IF HE EVEN TRIED TO LAY A FINGER ON ME.

DON'T LET HIM COME OUT. DON'T LET HIM COME OUT. DON'T LET HIM COME OUT.

AT THE LAKE

WILYNDA BARRY '86 ©

IT WAS IN JUNE WHEN WE SAW MRS. DAW-SON RUN OUT OF HER HOUSE INTO HER CAR AND PUT ON THE GAS SO HARD SHE LAYS A PATCH COMING AT US WE JUMP OUT OF THE WAY SHE TURNS DOWN THE HILL AND MAN SHE WAS GONE.

SCREECH!!

WATCH IT OR MY DAD'LL SUE YA!

I'M GONNA MAKE A CITIZENS ARREST ON HER!

HEY!

LADY DRIVER!

IT TURNS OUT SHE WAS DRIVING SO FAST BECAUSE OUR FRIEND DICKIE DAWSON HAD JUST DROWN AT THE LAKE WHERE ACCORDING TO MY MOTHER HE HAD NO BUSINESS BEING IN THE FIRST PLACE.

I DON'T KNOW WHAT SHE EXPECTED, LETTING HER CHILDREN GO GAL-LAVANTING WHERE EVER THEY PLEASE AND HER SITTING AROUND THE HOUSE WITH THAT NEW BOYFRIEND OF HERS. BUT I TELL YOU ONE THING IF I EVER CATCH EITHER ONE OF YOU AT THE LAKE YOU'LL BE SORRY YOU WERE EVER BORN.

ON THE DAY OF THE FUNERAL HARDLY NONE OF DICKIE'S FRIENDS WERE ALLOWED TO GO SO MOSTLY WE JUST SAT UP AT THE PLAYFIELD PULLING THE GRASS OUT AND TALKING ABOUT DICKIE. WE TRIED TO MAKE IT SOUND LIKE HE WAS THE BEST GUY OF EVERYONE. WE TRIED TO FORGET ANY TIME WE HAD BEEN MEAN TO HIM AND ESPECIALLY ANY TIME HE HAD BEEN MEAN TO US.

HE LET ME RIDE HIS BIKE.

HE SAT IN MY ROW IN ROOM 2.

HE CAME TO MY BIRTHDAY PARTY AND TOLD A JOKE.

HE SLUGGED ME IN THE BACK ONCE BUT I EARNED IT.

HE WAS KIND TO ANIMALS

THEN SOMEBODY SUGGESTS WE DO SOMETHING NICE FOR MRS. DAWSON TO SHOW HER HOW MUCH WE LIKE DICKIE AND WE DECIDE TO GO WAIT ON HER FRONT YARD AND WHEN SHE COMES HOME WE WILL ALL STAND UP AND SHOUT THE "2-4-6-8" CHEER SO SHE WILL ALWAYS KNOW.

CAR!

IS THAT THEIR CAR? THAT AIN'T THEIR CAR. IS IT?

THATS NOT THEIR CAR.

FALSE ALARM.

FAKE OUT.

THE WORST NIGHTMARE

BY LYNDA ALPHONSE BARRY 086

ONE NIGHT WHEN A BUNCH OF US WERE ON THE PORCH, DEENA WANTS TO TALK ABOUT THE BORINGIST THING IN THE WORLD WHICH WAS HER DREAMS. FIRST WE SAID **NO** UNTIL SHE SAID IT WAS A CONTEST FOR WHO HAD EVER HAD THE <u>WORST</u> NIGHTMARE.

BUT YOU HAVE TO SWEAR ON THE BIBLE TO TELL ONLY FOR-REAL NIGHTMARES. NO FAKE OUTS.

A COUPLE OF US START LYING RIGHT AWAY BY TELLING THE STORY OF "DIE MONSTER DIE" OR OTHER MOVIES THAT HAD THE MUMMY, ACID VATS, BLOOD DRIPPING FROM THE CEILING AND COMING ALIVE AFTER YOUR HEAD GOT CUT OFF.

THEN THIS LADY COMES RUNNIN' UP TO MY ROOM IN HER PAJAMAS AND SHE SAYS "YOU MUST HELP ME! MY HUSBAND TURNS OUT TO BE <u>DRACULA</u>" AND I SAY "WHAT NON-SENSE. THERE IS NO SUCH A THING AS A VAMPIRE!" O.K. THEN ITS THE NEXT DAY AND WE'RE IN ENGLAND...

WHEN IT COMES TO NICKY'S TURN HE SAYS "PASS." WE SAY "HOW COME?" AND HE SAYS IF HE EVEN THINKS ABOUT HIS WORST NIGHT-MARE HE HAS IT THAT NIGHT. IT'S ALWAYS THE SAME ONE, OVER AND OVER. WE WANT TO HEAR IT BUT HE KEEPS SAYING NO.

COME ON YOU GUYS, LAY OFF.

TELL US.
TELL US NICKY
TELL US.
TELL US NICKY
TELL US
TELL US NICKY
TELL US
TELL

FINALLY AFTER DUANE SAYS HE'S GONNA BASH NICKY'S HEAD IN IF HE DOESN'T TELL US, NICKY SAYS O.K.—YOU CAN TELL THAT HE'S ALMOST GOING TO CRY WHEN HE STARTS, AND SOME OF US FEEL SORT OF SORRY FOR HIM BUT WE WANT TO HEAR HIS NIGHTMARE REALLY BAD ANYWAY.

TELL IT MAN. AN' IF YOU START LYIN', I'LL SPOCK YOU.

HE'S GONNA TELL IT DUANE. LEAVE HIM ALONE.

YEAH. QUIT ACTIN' SO BIG.

WE ALL FELT PRETTY SCARED BECAUSE WE FIGURED WHAT WE WERE ABOUT TO HEAR WOULD BE THE HORRIBULIST THING IN THE WORLD. BUT ALL IT WAS WAS THAT NICKY DREAMS IT'S SUNDAY MORNING AND HIS MOM AND DAD (WHO ARE PRETTY MEAN) WANT TO TO INSPECT HIS ROOM, AND HE HEARS THEM COMING DOWN THE HALL AND SUDDENLY HE NOTICES HIS ROOM IS ALL FULL OF GARBAGE.

AND THERES NOTHIN' I CAN DO! THERES NO WAY I CAN CLEAN IT UP!! THEN MY DOOR OPENS AND I WANT TO TELL THEM IT'S NOT MY FAULT BUT NO SOUND COMES OUT.

AND THEN I WAKE UP.

WE ALL THOUGHT IT WAS A PRETTY BOGUS DREAM. BIG DEAL IF YOUR ROOM IS FULL OF GARBAGE. DUANE SAID WE SHOULD ALL GET TO GIVE NICKY ONE SOCK EACH FOR EVEN GETTING OUR HOPES UP. NICKY DIDN'T SAY NOTHING.

GOOD DOG

TOLD BY GAIL F. • MAJOR EMBELLISHMENTS BY LYNDA BARRY ©87

ONE TIME IN THE SUMMER I HAD THIS DREAM OF MAKING FRIENDS WITH THIS ONE DOG IN OUR ALLEY NAMED TIMMY WHO EVERYONE WAS TOTALLY SCARED OF BECAUSE HE WAS A WILD TIED UP KIND OF DOG WHO SOMETIMES GOT LOOSE AND WOULD RIP GIANT HOLES IN YOUR PANTS AND ALSO TRY TO DANCE WITH YOU.

RUN FOR IT MAN!! TIMMY'S LOOSE!

IT TOOK ABOUT TWO HOURS BUT HOW I DID IT WAS BY TALKING TO HIM AS SWEET AS IF HE WERE THE BABY JESUS AND GIVING HIM BALONGA AND MOVING TOWARD HIM IN PERFECT SLOW MOTION. WHEN HE FINALLY LET ME PET HIM I FELT LIKE I WAS THE WINNER OF THE WHOLE WORLD.

GOOD BOY GOOD DOG GOOD TIMMY

NICE DOG

YEAH, THAT'S A SWEET LITTLE BOY

WANT ME TO SING YOU ANOTHER SONG BOY?

♪ WHATS IT ALLA BOUT ALFEE WHATS IT ALLA BOUT ALFEE ♪

I JUST KEPT PETTING HIM AND PETTING HIM AND SINGING HIM A MILLION SONGS LIKE "THE HILLS ARE ALIVE" AND "RICE-A-RONI THE SAN FRANCISCO TREAT." MY MAIN PROBLEM CAME WHEN I TRIED TO GET UP, TIMMY TRIED TO BITE ME. IF I TRIED TO <u>MOVE</u> HE'D START GROWLING. HE WOULDN'T LET ME LEAVE. I STARTED YELLING FOR HELP. I YELLED ABOUT SIX HUNDRED TIMES BEFORE MY COUSIN MARLYS CAME.

MARLYS GOT THE PLAN OF GETTING A HOT DOG AND FLINGING IT TO THE SIDE SO WHEN TIMMY WENT TO GET IT I COULD ESCAPE, AND HER PLAN WORKED. WHEN I GOT BACK TO THE YARD I STARTED SHAKING AND SHAKING AND I COULDN'T STOP. WHEN I TRIED TO TALK I STARTED CRYING FOR NO REASON. AND THEN OF ALL THINGS, MARLYS, MY DREADED COUSIN, PUT HER ARM AROUND ME.

BIG BIRTHDAY

BY LYNDA BARRY © 1986

IT GOT PASSED AROUND THAT KENNETH WAS GOING TO HAVE A GIANT BIRTHDAY PARTY ON SATURDAY AND WHO STARTED THE STORY WAS OF COURSE KENNETH. WE BELIEVED IN THE PARTY PART BUT NOT ALL THE OTHER JUNK HE SAID LIKE FIRETRUCKS COMING TO GIVE US FREE RIDES.

NO WAY MAN.

BETCHA.

BETCHA A MILLION BUCKS.

ALL THE BOYS WERE INVITED TO SPEND THE NIGHT FRIDAY NIGHT SLEEPING IN A BIG TENT KENNETH'S DAD SET UP. THE PARTY WAS SUPPOSED TO BEGIN AT WHENEVER KENNETH SAID ON SATURDAY WITH ALL THE M+M PANCAKES YOU EVER WANTED. GIRLS WEREN'T INVITED. NO GIRLS ALLOWED.

AND MY DAD SAYS WE CAN BRING THE T.V. ON A STENSHUN CORD OUT IN THE TENT TO WATCH NIGHTMARE THEATER. IT'S GONNA BE THE BEST DAY OF MY LIFE!

WHEN FRIDAY NIGHT CAME, DEENA AND I GOT PERMISSION TO SLEEP OUT ON THE PORCH AT MY HOUSE. WE COULD HEAR ALL THE BOYS DOWN AT KENNETH'S BEHAVING LIKE WILD INDIANS A WHOLE BLOCK AWAY. WE DECIDED WE HAD BETTER GO DOWN AND SPY ON THEM.

JUST AS WE GOT THERE WE HAD TO HIDE IN THE BUSHES FAST BECAUSE OUT COMES KENNETH'S DAD SLAMMING THE SCREEN DOOR AND YELLING POINTING A BOTTLE OF BEER AT THE TENT AND YELLING THAT THE RACKET WAS DRIVING HIM BATSHIT SO CAN IT AND NEXT TIME HE COMES OUT IT WILL BE KENNETH'S LITTLE BUTT DO YOU HEAR?

IT KEPT THEM QUIET, REAL QUIET,
BECAUSE EVERYONE KNEW KENNETH'S
DAD WAS THE HARDEST HITTER OF ANY-
ONE'S DAD. WE SAT IN THE BUSHES AND
TRIED TO SPY ON WHAT THE BOYS
WERE TALKING ABOUT WHEN ALL OF
A SUDDEN WE COULD HEAR KENNETH'S
MOM AND DAD YELLING AT EACH
OTHER FROM INSIDE THE HOUSE. THEN
STUFF WAS BREAKING IN THERE AND
KENNETH'S MOTHER YELLS SHE'LL
CALL THE COPS AND THAT'S WHEN
KENNETH TURNS UP THE T.V. THEY GOT
IN THE TENT TO FULL BLAST.

START
RUNNING!

AND THEN HIS DAD COMES OUT.

HOME AND FAMILY

Naturally he had got ahold of some PLAYBOYS which made him the president of all the boys. Where he hid them, was at the FORT.

READY, MEN?

YES, YOUR ROYAL PRESIDENT, SIR.

MISS JULY

Pretty soon he was considered a bad element and you were automatically grounded if your mother caught you playing with him. PARENTS CALLED HIM "THE RING LEADER"

IF WE PLAY WITH YOU, MOM SAID SHE'D CREAM US.

LIKE I EVEN CARE!

BIG DEAL YA SISSIES!

THROUGHOUT THE Days OF HiS CHILDhood he remained fearless and a BORN Hellraiser. The ONLY Thing he was Scared of, was Looking at aLFred E. Newman's Face. WHY I DON'T KNOW.

Eventually, Like anyone else, he turned 16. This Shed a whole new LIGHT on things, Like a CAR. WHICH he took OFF in.

VA Room!

SCREECH

MY TEENAGE BROTHA

BY LYNDA BARRY © 84

PUH-PUL HAZE ALL THR

> SHUT UP AND. GET OUT OF MY ROOM

CHIPS AHOY

I remember one time I told my brother that the music of Jimi Hendrix was "ungentle". At the time, he was high on grass.

He was a real hit with girls but not with their mothers. Often he was making out. Since I was older I warned him of unwanted pregnancy.

> SHUT UP AND GET OUT OF MY ROOM.

BRUCE LE

He went through what you might call a rebelious period which included crimminal acts, the WORLD OF DRUGS, music of the electric guitar and a 1965 MUSTANG CONVERTABLE. OUTWARDLY, HE seemed happy, but I knew better.

MIKE, I WANT TO SHARE WITH YOU. LET'S RAP ABOUT YOUR FEELINGS.

I SAID GET OUT, MAN.

The night of his HIGHSCHOOL GRADUATION, He took LSD AND WANDERED NAKED through a FOUNTAIN, expressing HIMSELF.

CHECK OUT DUDE!

DUDE CRAZY!

On the way to the police Station, I was trying to explain to mom the concept of "DOING YOUR OWN thing" to provide understanding toward my Brother's ACTIONS. However she was not in the right space at that time.

I encouraged my brother to expand his intellectual HORIZONS. He, However, had his own ideas and went to work in a tire Store. Eventually He had a Red CORVette. He is SO materialistic And it worries me.

HER NAME WAS NEENEE AND SHE WAS EVERYONE'S FAVORITE BECAUSE YOU COULD MAKE HER SO MAD THAT HER FACE WOULD GET RED, BIG LINES WOULD COME OUT ON HER NECK AND DROOL WOULD OCCUR. MOM SAID YOU SHOULD FEEL SORRY FOR THAT LITTLE GIRL BUT WE SAID FORGET IT.
SLOBBERGIRL! SLOBBERGIRL! SLOBBERGIRL!
UH-OH! RUN FOR IT! HERE SHE COMES!

MOM SAID "SHE'S SICK" BUT SHE LOOKED O.K. TO US, JUST UGLY. EVEN HER OWN BROTHERS AND SISTERS SAID SO. BUT NEENEE'S MOTHER SAID NEENEE WAS THE ONE THE ANGELS LIKED BEST. WE ALL THOUGHT "NO WAY!"
HOLD STILL HONEY, FOR MAMA CAN COMB YOUR PRETTY HAIR.
WHO DOES MAMA LOVE?
WHO IS JESUS'S SPECIAL LITTLE LAMB?

THEN ONE TIME NEENEE GOT LOST. SHE WAS LOST SO LONG THEY HAD TO CALL THE POLICE. WE WERE ALL LOOKING AND LOOKING. WE WERE ALL YELLING HER NAME. THEN THEY SAID ON THE TELEPHONE THEY FOUND HER. SOME TEENAGERS HAD PUSHED HER DOWN A HOLE.

THANK GOD SHE IS SAFE!

OH MY CHRIST!

OH MY LORD IN HEAVEN!

WHEN THE POLICE BROUGHT HER BACK HE HELD HER UP TO SHOW US SHE WAS O.K. AND SUDDENLY EVERYONE OF US STARTED CRYING AND I DON'T EVEN KNOW WHY.

TWICE AS BIG

BY L·Y·N·D·A 101.5° B·A·R·R·Y ©1986

I WAS TWICE AS BIG AS MY SISTER, BUT ONLY HALF AS UGLY. THE STORY GOES THAT ON THE DAY WE WERE BORN I CAME OUT SO BIG THAT NO BODY COULD EVEN BELIEVE THERE WAS SOMEONE ELSE IN THERE WITH ME. IRENE PRACTICALLY HAD TO CRAWL OUT ON HER OWN BECAUSE NO ONE HAD ANY REASON TO CHECK FOR MORE.

WHAT IS GOING ON!

WELL I'LL BE A MONKEYS UNCLE!

IRENE WAS LOUSY LOOKING FROM THE WORD GO. PEOPLE WOULD SEE US AND TRY TO THINK OF SOMETHING DECENT TO SAY ABOUT HER WHICH WAS USUALLY "WHAT A UNIQUE FACE!". IN REGARDS TO ME IT WAS THE USUAL "WHAT A CUTE BABY" BUT IRENE NEVER GOT THE WORD CUTE. I'LL TELL YOU ONE THING, UGLY CHILDREN ARE A EMBARRISMENT TO EVERYONE CONCERNED.

TWINS?!! YOU'RE KIDDING!

WHY... AREN'T THEY... UH, A WONDER!

AT LEAST YOU CAN TELL THEM APART!

IN ALL THE MOVIES OR BOOKS ABOUT UGLY LITTLE GIRLS THEY ALWAYS GOT BEAUTIFUL BY THE END. HOW THEY DID THIS WAS BY HAVING A GOLDEN HEART INSIDE OF THEIR REPULSIVE BODIES. I TRIED TO EXPLAIN TO IRENE THAT BEING THE NICEST GIRL ON EARTH EVEN TO THE BOYS THAT PUSHED HER OVER DURING RECESS WAS HER ONLY PRAYER OF EVER LOOKING APEALLING. SHE WOULD TRY FOR A WHILE BUT BASICALLY SHE DEVELOPED A CRUMMY PERSONALITY INSTEAD.

HOW MANY TIMES DO I HAVE TO TELL YOU? WHEN THEY SHOVE YOU OVER DON'T GO KICKIN' THEM BETWEEN THEIR LEGS!

YOU GOTTA JUST ACCEPT IT AND MAKE IT SO THEY FEEL ROTTEN ABOUT IT.

BY THE TIME WE WERE IN HIGH SCHOOL, SHE WAS THE MEANEST PERSON PROBABLY ANYONE HAD EVER KNOWN. THATS WHEN I REALIZED SHE HAD TOTALLY GIVEN UP ON THE IDEA OF A HAPPY ENDING.

WHAT KILLS ME IS IF YOU HAD BEEN NICER TO PEOPLE YOU WOULD HAVE PROBABLY BEEN BEAUTIFUL BY NOW! BUT NO. YOU HAD TO GO AND RUIN YOUR ONLY CHANCE IN LIFE.

WELL, TOUGH LUCK IS ALL I HAVE TO SAY!

TRAIN RIDE

By LYNDA — I SMOKE OLD STOGIES I HAVE FOUND — BARRY © 1986

"PSST. WAKE UP MAN!" MY BROTHER SAYS TOUCHING MY FOOT AND YANKING ON IT. IT'S PITCH DARK, THEN SOME CAR LIGHTS SLIDE ACROSS THE WALL AND ONTO HIS FACE AND I SEE HE LOOKS SCARED. "ERNIE'S GONE. HE JUST WENT OUT THE BACK DOOR. WE'RE DEAD." ERNIE WAS OUR LITTLE BROTHER.

PRETTY SOON I CAN JUST BARELY SEE ERNIE THE STUPID IDIOT DUCKING UNDER THIS HOLE IN THE FENCE THAT GOES TO THE TRAIN TRACKS. I RUN TO CATCH UP BUT I DON'T YELL HIS NAME BECAUSE NOW HE'S UNDER THE WOODEN BRIDGE AND THERE'S WINOS ASLEEP AND WHO KNOWS WHAT THEY WOULD DO TO A DIPSHIT SIX YEAR OLD STANDING THERE IN HIS PAJAMAS.

WHEN OUR MOM LEFT SHE TOLD US SHE LOVED US AND FELT LIKE SHE WAS DYING OR SOMETHING AND ERNIE WAS THE ONLY ONE DUMB ENOUGH TO BELIEVE HER. HE DON'T EVEN KNOW WHERE SHE WENT BECAUSE NO ONE KNOWS. ALL HE KNOWS IS THAT SHE RODE THE TRAIN AND THAT IF HE CAN GET ON THE TRAIN HE'LL FIND HER. STUPID KID THINKS THERE'S ONLY ONE TRAIN IN THE WHOLE WIDE WORLD, YOU KNOW?

WHEN HE FINALLY SEES ME HE DON'T EVEN RUN AND I DON'T EVEN CREAM HIM. WE WALK UNDER THE BRIDGE AND BACK THROUGH THE FENCE AND WHEN HE HOLDS MY HAND, HIS FINGERS ARE SO SMALL I WANT TO SCREAM. I WISH I WEREN'T TOO OLD TO BAWL MY HEAD OFF ANYMORE.
I WISH I WAS OLD ENOUGH TO RIDE AWAY ON SOME GODDAMN TRAIN.

BRANDED

By Lynda Big Screen Barry

MY SISTER CAME HOME FROM SCHOOL AN' SLUGGED ME FOR JUST STANDING THERE. SHE SAID SHE HATED ME AND EVERYTHING ESPECIALLY OUR MOM AND OUR DAD AND OUR HOUSE.

THEN SHE TURNED AROUND I SAW SHE HAD GRASS STAINS ON HER BACK. AND MY SISTER NEVER LAID ON THE GROUND.

NORMALLY I HATED MY SISTER AS MUCH AS SHE HATED ME, AND NORMALLY WHO EVEN CARES ABOUT HOW CRUDDY SHE ACTS. MOM SAYS ONCE YOU'RE ABOUT 15 YOU TURN TO A STUPID IDIOT AND THATS FOR SURE. BUT NOW SHE'S IN THE BATHROOM, RUNNING WATER AND CRYING LIKE SHE CRIED WHEN OUR DOG GOT KILLED. I SIT BY THE DOOR AND WAIT.

LATER WHEN OUR MOM COMES HOME, AUTO-
MATICALLY SHE'S YELLING AT MICHELLE
AS USUAL AND I WANT TO TELL HER "MOM
DON'T YELL AT HER TONIGHT. CAN'T YOU
TELL SOMETHING'S WRONG?" BUT HOW
COULD YOU EVER SAY THAT TO YOUR MOM?
SO I BREAK A GLASS AND A PLATE AND
FINALLY SHE'S YELLING AT ME.

I'M ASLEEP AND THE BED IS MOVING AND
I OPEN MY EYES AND SEE MICHELLE
ON HER KNEES AT THE WINDOW CRYING
AND SHAKING HER HEAD NO! NO! NO! AND
I LOOK OUT THE WINDOW AND THERE'S
TWO BOYS, TWO TEENAGERS LEANING
ON A CAR AND LAUGHING. ONE EVEN YELLS
HER NAME "C'MON MICHELLE" AND BEFORE
MY SISTER KNOCKS ME BACK ON TO THE
BED YOU CAN BET I MADE THE FINGER AT
THEM. BOTH OF THEM.

GOING BAD

BY LINDA ONE MEATBALL BARRY © 1986

BY THE TIME YOU'RE TWELVE OR SOMETHING YOUR OWN STREET YOU KNOW SO WELL IT ABOUT MAKES YOU WANT TO BARF JUST TO WALK DOWN IT SOMETIMES. YOU KNOW EVERYTHING THAT EVER HAPPENED AND EVERYTHING THAT'S GONNA HAPPEN. I MEAN YOU WANNA SCREAM.

YOU USUALLY HAVE A COUPLE OF FRIENDS THAT FEEL THE SAME WAY SO JUST NATURALLY YOU'RE GOING TO GO SOMEWHERE THATS EXCITING TO YOU. THAT'S SOMETHING NOBODY CAN HELP DOING EVENTUALLY.

AND MAYBE SUDDENLY SOMETHING AWFUL
HAPPENS BECAUSE AWFUL THINGS JUST DO
SOMETIMES AND AFTERWARDS YOU TURN THE
CORNER AND THERE'S YOUR BEAUTIFUL
STREET. YOUR BEAUTIFUL DUMB LITTLE STREET.
AND YOU SEE YOUR MOM AND YOU WANT TO
TELL HER WHY YOU'RE HUGGING HER EXCEPT
YOU KNOW SHE'D KILL YOU IF YOU TOLD HER
SO YOU JUST LET HER THINK YOU'VE GONE
CRAZY.

AND THE NEXT DAY YOU WAKE UP AND
YOU GO TO THE WINDOW TO SEE YOUR
BEAUTIFUL STREET AGAIN BUT INSTEAD
IT LOOKS WORSE TO YOU THAN EVER BEFORE
AND IT SCARES YOU BECAUSE —

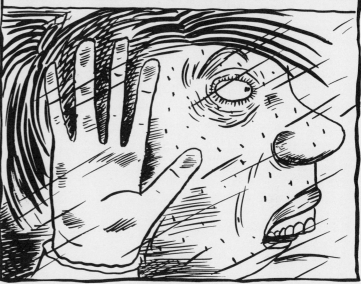

MAYBONNE'S ROOM

By LYNDA MUDDY HEADED BARRY © 1987

THE MAIN TEENAGER OF MY LIFE WAS MY COUSIN MARLYS'S SISTER, MAYBONNE WHO'S NERVES WE GOT ON. SHE WOULD ALWAYS LEAN DOWN ABOUT ONE INCH FROM YOUR FACE AND YELL "BUG OFF, MAN!" WHEN YOU FOLLOWED HER AROUND. BUT THIS NEVER STOPPED HER FROM BEING MY IDOL.

THE ONE THING WE WERE NEVER SUPPOSED TO DO WAS GO IN HER BEDROOM WHICH WE DID ANYWAY. IT WAS WORTH HAVING HER YELL AT US, FOR IT WAS THE COOLEST PLACE I EVER SAW. HOW COME TEENAGERS CAN DECORATE EVERYTHING SO PERFECT?

SHE HAD HER OWN RADIO AND WE WOULD SPY ON HER ACTING OUT SONGS IN FRONT OF THE MIRROR. IF A SAD SONG CAME ON SHE'D GET RIGHT UP CLOSE TO THE MIRROR AND TRY TO SEE HOW SHE LOOKED WHEN SHE WAS CRYING. OTHER TIMES SHE'D PULL HER SHIRT UP AND STARE AT HER BRA FOR NO REASON.

ABOUT THE BEST NIGHT OF MY LIFE WAS WHEN MAYBONNE WAS GROUNDED FOR A WEEK SO WE WERE HER ONLY CHOICE OF WHO TO HANG AROUND WITH. ONE NIGHT SHE EVEN LET US SLEEP IN HER ROOM. SHE TAUGHT US THE GREAT DANCE OF "THE HITCH HIKER" AND WE ALL THREE DID IT IN A LINE IN FRONT OF THE MIRROR. AND I WILL NEVER FORGET THAT NIGHT BECAUSE MAYBONNE KEPT THE RADIO ON AND IT WAS THE FIRST TIME I EVER HEARD MUSIC WHEN YOU'RE JUST LAYING THERE WITH YOUR COUSINS IN THE PITCH DARK.

THE NEW HOUSE

BY YOUR FRIEND, DEACON LYNDA BARRY © 1986

WHEN WE FIRST LAID EYES ON THE NEW HOUSE, MY BROTHER AND I STARTED BAWLING AND WOULDN'T GET OUT OF THE CAR. MY MOM TURNED AROUND AND SAID AT US "DON'T START." BUT IT WAS TOO LATE.

WE ARE DOOMED.

IT WAS A OLD UGLY HOUSE THAT NOBODY WAS LIVING IN. WE HAD BEEN LIVING AT OUR COUSIN MARLYSES HOUSE AND I THOUGHT ANYTHING WOULD BE BETTER THAN SLEEPING IN THE BED WITH MARLYS AND SMELLING THAT TERRIBLE ODOR OF THEIR FOOD BUT I WAS WRONG. MARLYSES CAR WAS BEHIND OURS AND WHEN SHE SAW OUR HOUSE NATURALLY SHE STARTED LAUGHING SO NATURALLY I HAD TO GET OUT OF THE CAR AND SLUG HER.

THATS MY MAMA'S HOUSE YOU'RE LAUGHIN' AT, BUTT FACE.

YOW!

AUNTIE GLADYS!

WE WENT UP THE STAIRS AND THEY HAD THE SOUND OF NIGHTMARE THEATER. SO DID THE DOOR. THERE WERE BROKEN WINDOWS WHICH MARLYS SAID EQUALS IT'S HAUNTED. I TOLD HER TO GET LOST. THEN WE WENT INTO THE BATHROOM AND SAW THE DEAD BUGS IN THE SINK. WE SAW THE DEAD BUGS IN THE BATHTUB. THEN MARLYS TURNS ON THE FAUCET AND JET RED BLOOD POURS OUT. WE RAN OUT SCREAMING AND GRAB ONTO MY MOM WHICH ONLY MAKES HER MADDER.

PICK ME UP MAMA!

PLEASE!

IT'S A EMER-GENCY!

AUNTIE GLADYS!

WE'RE GONNA DIE!

TIDE

MY MOM TELLS US ITS JUST RUST NOT NOBODY'S BLOOD BUT SHE'S ONLY SAYING THAT FOR HOW CAN THERE BE LIQUID RUST? THEN I HAD TO DO THE WORST THING OF MY LIFE WHICH WAS TO BEG MARLYS TO LET ME STAY WITH HER SOMEMORE. SHE MADE ME PROMISE TO BE HER SLAVE FOR LIFE AND CALL HER YOUR HIGHNESS. I SAID O.K.   BUT MY MOM SAID NO, I HAD TO STAY.

MAR-LYS!

COMIN'

NOW!

O.K.

WELL.

TOUGH LUCK ABOUT MOVIN' INNA HOUSE WHERE BLOOD COMES OUTTA THE FAUCETS.

IT'S RUST.

OLD Lady

BY LYNDA SLIP 'N' SLIDE BARRY ©1986

ON THE CORNER UP THE HILL WAS THE HOUSE OF THIS ONE OLD LADY MRS. KUBEL. HER HUSBAND DIED WAY BEFORE I EVEN GOT BORN AND HER KIDS WERE DEAD TOO FROM A WAR THAT WAS TOO BAD TO EVEN TELL US ABOUT. EVERYBODY, EVEN MY MOM WHO NEVER FELT SORRY FOR PRACTICALLY NO ONE, FELT SORRY FOR MRS. KUBEL.

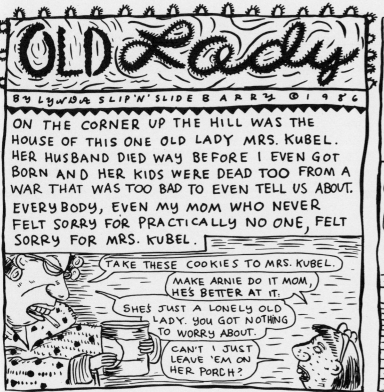

TAKE THESE COOKIES TO MRS. KUBEL.

MAKE ARNIE DO IT MOM, HE'S BETTER AT IT.

SHE'S JUST A LONELY OLD LADY. YOU GOT NOTHING TO WORRY ABOUT.

CAN'T I JUST LEAVE 'EM ON HER PORCH?

SHE SCARED ME AND MY FRIENDS BECAUSE IF YOU EVER GOT CLOSE TO HER SHE WANTED TO TOUCH YOU AND HUG YOU LIKE YOU WERE A BABY OR SOMETHING. AND IF YOU LET HER DO IT, MRS. KUBEL WOULD SOMETIMES START CRYING AND SQUEEZING YOU TIGHTER AND IT FELT LIKE YOU BOTH WERE GOING TO DIE IN SLOW-MOTION.

VY IST YOUR PAPA SO LATE?

VY IST HE NOT COMING BECK YET?

MRS KUBEL I GOTTA GO OK MRS. KUBEL?

VY IST PAPA NOT BECK HERE YET WIT MY BABIES?

I REALLY GOTTA GO MRS. KUBEL PLEASE OK?

VERE ARE MY BABIES? VERE IST MIE HUSBAND?

OH MAN MRS KUBEL PLEASE I GOTTA GO NOW.

EVERYBODY IN THE NEIGHBORHOOD HAD TO GO OVER TO MRS. KUBEL'S TO HELP HER WITH SOMETHING BUT NOT EVEN <u>ONE</u> OF OUR MOMS AND DADS EVER CAME OVER. ALWAYS JUST THE KIDS. SO THEY NEVER SAW WHAT WE SAW AND THEY NEVER FELT LIKE WE FELT AFTER WARDS: THAT FEELING OF NO MATTER WHAT YOU DID, THERE WAS NOTHING YOU COULD DO. I MEAN, YOU'RE JUST A KID, YOU KNOW?

MOM PLEASE DON'T MAKE ME GO OVER THERE. PLEASE MAMA.

WHAT A SELFISH CHILD! YOU WON'T EVEN GO VISIT AN OLD LONELY WOMAN TO SEE IF SHE NEEDS ANYTHING!

COME WITH ME MAMA. I'LL GO IF YOU COME WITH ME, O.K.?

ABSOLUTELY <u>NOT</u>! NOW GO GET YOUR JACKET AND GET OVER THERE!

FINALLY ONE DAY DICKIE NELLEMS HAD TO BRING SOMETHING OVER TO MRS. KUBEL AND IT TURNED OUT SHE WAS JUST LAYING THERE ON THE FLOOR DEAD. SUDDENLY ALL OUR MOMS AND DADS WERE OVER THERE INSIDE MRS. KUBEL'S HOUSE SAYING TO US KIDS "KEEP AWAY!" "STAY OUT!" LIKE WE WEREN'T OLD ENOUGH TO HANDLE IT. BUT ALL OF US KNEW THAT WHAT THEY WERE LOOKING AT WAS <u>NOTHING</u> COMPARED TO WHAT WE HAD SEEN.

I WANT YOU AND THE REST OF THE KIDS OUT OF HERE! THIS HAS NOTHING TO DO WITH YOU! NOW GO ON!

AND FOR GODSAKES LEAVE THE POLICEMEN ALONE!

THEY DON'T HAVE TIME FOR YOUR SILLY QUESTIONS!

NOW GET GOING! GO ON!

THIS IS NO PLACE FOR KIDS RIGHT NOW.

AFTER SHE WAS DONE SHE'D MAKE US STAND NEXT TO EACH OTHER AND SHE'D LOOK AT US AND TILT HER HEAD BACK AND FORTH LIKE A GERMAN SHEPARD HEARING A WEIRD NOISE, WATCHING FOR SOME HAIR SHE HAD MISSED. WHEN WE WERE FINALLY TOTALLY BALD SHE'D PUT A RIBBON ON US.

AUNTIE ARDIS SCOTCH TAPE LOOKS FUNNY ON A HEAD.

NONSENSE! SCOTCH TAPE IS TOTALLY INVISIBLE!

BESIDES! HOW ELSE CAN YOU EXPECT TO HOLD THESE ADORABLE RIBBONS ON?!

BE STILL MARLYS!

WHEN I GROW UP I'M GONNA GROW MY HAIR DOWN PAST MY BUTT.

SO EVEN THOUGH IT WAS A MILLION DEGREES OUTSIDE ME AND MARLYS WORE SKI JACKETS BECAUSE IT WAS THE ONLY THING WE HAD WITH HOODS. AND EVEN THOUGH WE HATED EACH OTHER WE SORT OF FELT LIKE BEST FRIENDS UNTIL WE GOT SOME HAIR AGAIN.

HEYA STUPES. DONCHA EVEN KNOW IT'S SUMMER?

SO?

BIG DEAL, MAN.

AIN'T YOU GUYS HOT?

NOPE.

NOPE.

Fine Dining

By chef LYNDA LA BARREE © 1986

ALTHOUGH HARDLY ANYBODY HAD EVER GONE TO A GREAT RESTAURANT, ALL OF US HAD OPINIONS ON WHAT WAS A EXCELLENT MEAL. FOR MY BROTHER IT WAS 2 CHICKEN POT PIES WITH COLD SPAGHETTI-O'S RIGHT OUT OF THE CAN. I PREFERRED THE DELICATE TASTE OF FRIED BALONEY AND MAYONAISE ON SUNBEAM BREAD.

LEAVE IT IN THE CAN PLEASE

ETTI-O'S

MILK GLASS MUST HAVE HANDLE

INITIALS CARVED ON PIE

SOLE UTENSIL

T.V. TRAY: "A MUST"

FRY BALONEY UNTIL IT HUMPS UP. BURN EDGES. HIDE FRYING PAN UNDER BED SO MOM WON'T CREAM YOU FOR THE BLACK MARKS THAT YOU CAN'T SCRUB OUT.

AT EVERYONE'S HOUSE THEIR FAMILY ATE AT LEAST <u>ONE</u> THING THAT WAS SCARY.

DEENA'S

MUSTARD AND ONION AND RELISH SANDWICHES

THE TWINS

JELLY ON SPAGHETTI

OUR HOUSE

"DINOU-GOUAAN" (A.K.A "MIDNIGHT MEAT" and "BLACK OUT")

MARLYS

"BAGOUNG" (SCARY PINK FISH CONDIMENT THAT THE SMELL WOULD MAKE YOU START RUNNING)

WALTER'S

SARDINES AND COOL WHIP

(HE ATE THIS FOR SHOW OFF ONLY)

DICKY'S

FRIED PIG GUTS

OUR MAIN OPINIONS, HOWEVER, REGARDED THE WORLD OF DESSERTS. FOR EXAMPLE EVERYONE AGREED ANYTHING TASTED THE BEST WHEN YOU ATE IT IN YOUR CLASS ROOM DURING A HALLOWEEN OR VALENTINES PARTY. EVEN THE WORST KOOL-AID WAS SIMPLY DELICIOUS IF IT WAS IN A PAPER CUP ON YOUR DESK WITH A CUPCAKE. (ESPECIALLY IF THE CUPCAKE WAS IN A <u>BLUE</u> PAPER HOLDER. THE WORST CUPCAKE HOLDER WAS THE YELLOW.) (YELLOW WAS ALWAYS BAD DUE TO P.)

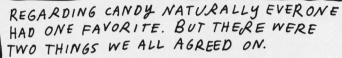

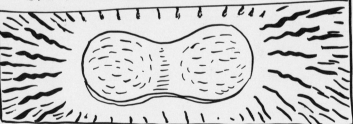

REGARDING CANDY NATURALLY EVERONE HAD ONE FAVORITE. BUT THERE WERE TWO THINGS WE ALL AGREED ON.

① CHUNKYS WERE A TOTAL RIP OFF

② THE WORST CANDY KNOWN TO THE ENTIRE UNIVERSE IS THOSE ORANGE MARSHMELLOW "PEANUTS" ESPECIALLY WHEN THEY HAVE BEEN SITTING IN A BOWL SO LONG THEY HAVE DUST ON THEM BUT YOUR MOM FORCES YOU TO EAT IT BECAUSE IT WAS A OLD PERSON WHO GAVE IT TO YOU.

THE BABYSITTER

BY LYNDA -THROW THE SWITCH- BARRY © 1986

IF YOU'RE GOING TO HAVE A BABYSITTER YOU MIGHT AS WELL HAVE A **MIDGET** WHO DRIVES A GREAT BIG OLD GREEN STATION WAGON WITH REAL LIVING MOSS GROWING IN IT FOR YOUR BABYSITTER, IN OUR OPINION. AT FIRST HIS LOOKS MAY SCARE YOU BECAUSE HE ONLY GOTS ABOUT 3 TEETH LEFT AND SOME FINGERS ARE GONE BUT LET ME TELL YOU EVENTUALLY YOU WILL JUST LOVE HIM.

HELLO DARLING!

FOR ONE THING, HE IS ALWAYS BRINGING OVER THOSE BIG BAGS OF DOUGHNUT HOLES WHICH NO ONE CAN RESIST. THE OTHER THING IS HE INVENTS GOOD GAMES SUCH AS "YOU GET BACK THERE" WHERE HE THROWS YOUR GRANDMA'S SLIPPER AT YOU AND GENERALLY ACTS LIKE A LADY RUNNING AROUND WITH A HIGH VOICE AND MAKING YOU LAUGH UNTIL YOU PRACTICALLY STRANGLE OR SOMETHING.

MY GOLLY!

WHY ARE YOU RUNNING PROM ME?! I AM SO BERY BEAUTIPAL TODAY DARLING!

I AM A BERY BEAUTPAL ONE TODAY DARLING!

MY HAIRS IS ESO PREETY!

MY LOBLY PIGURE IS PABULOUS, NO?

THE MAN NEXT DOOR SOMETIMES SHAKES HIS CIGARETTE AT YOU SAYING "IT'S A DAMN GOOD THING THAT GUY'S RELATED TO YOU OR I'D HAVE THE COPS OVER HERE TO PUT HIS PANSY ASS IN A SLING IN NO TIME" AND THE WAY HE SAYS IT MAKES YOU GO OVER TO HIS YARD AT NIGHT AND PEE ON ALL HIS FLOWERS.

YER MA, SAYS HES YOUR UNCLE BUT I DON'T BLAME YOU ONE BIT FOR DENYIN' IT, KID.

THE TIME YOUR BABY SITTER COMES OVER WITH STITCHES ON HIS FACE AND WALKING SORE AND YOUR MOM TELLS YOU THAT IN GENERAL EVEN THE BEST GUY IN THE WORLD CAN GET BEAT UP JUST BECAUSE HE LIKES BEING A LADY, THAT'S WHAT GIVES YOU THE PROBLEMS.

KNOW WHAT ME AN' TIM ARE GONNA DO? WE'RE GONNA FIND THOSE GUYS AND JUST BASH THEIR BRAINS OUT FOR THIS, MAN.

YUP. THATS RIGHT.

THE NIGHT WE ALL GOT SICK

BY LYNDA "BAD TO THE BONEY BUTT" BARRY © 1986

MINE'S BIGGER!

IS NOT, YA LIAR!

IS SO YA DOPE.

IT ALL STARTED AT THE PARADE WHERE ALL OF US GOT TO PICK ONE THING. ME AND MY BROTHER BOTH PICKED COTTON CANDY. MY COUSIN FREDDIE PICKED A BLUE SNO-KONE. MY OTHER COUSIN MARLYS PICKED A HOT DOG WHICH WAS A PERFECTLY STUPID PICK.

LATER WE ALL GOT TO SLEEP IN MY COUSIN'S HOUSE IN THE FRONT ROOM BUT NO HORSEPLAY. NONE OF US FELT LIKE IT ANYWAY BECAUSE WE ALL HATED EACH OTHER'S GUTS. ESPECIALLY ME AND MARLYS. SO WE ALL HAD OUR OWN TERRITORY WHICH WAS OFF LIMITS.

"LAND OF MARLYS" ALSO KNOWN AS "BUTT ISLAND"

"LAND OF FREDDIE" ALSO KNOWN AS "SMELL-O-RAMA" AND "STINK-WORLD"

"LAND OF MY BROTHER" ALSO KNOWN AS TOTAL RETARDED UNIVERSE AND GALAXY

MY LAND WHICH WAS GORGEOUS AND SMELLED LIKE PERFUME FROM FRANCE

MARLYS STARTED IT BY SITTING UP AND BARFING AND PRETTY SOON ALL OF US WERE. MY BROTHER RAN TO GET AUNT SYLVIA AND SLIPPED AND FELL AND THREW-UP. NONE OF US COULD EVEN LAUGH. EVENTUALLY AUNT SYLVIA AND UNCLE TED HELPED US AND TOOK TURNS ROCKING US IN THEIR BIG ROCKER AS SOON AS WE COULD STAND IT.

FER CRISSAKE TED GET YOUR BUTT OVER HERE. MY ARMS ARE NUMB.

WHAT THE HELL TIME IS IT ANYWAY?

HOLY BALLS.

AFTER THAT NIGHT WE ALL HAD A SECRET WEAPON AGAINST EACH OTHER. ALL YOU HAD TO DO WAS SAY THE WORDS "SNO-KONE" TO FREDDIE AND HE'D PRACTICALLY START CRYING. MY BROTHER'S AND MINE WAS THE SAME SO WE NEVER USED IT. BUT MARLYS WOULD CALL UP OUR HOUSE AND ASK FOR ME AND WHEN I SAID HELLO SHE'D WHISPER "THE SMELL OF COTTON CANDY."
BUT EVEN JUST A DRAWING OF A HOTDOG WOULD MAKE HER BAWL. WHICH IS WHY I GOT TO BE SUCH A GOOD ARTIST.

DEAR MARLYS, DOES THIS LOOK FAMILIAR?

PIXIE

BY LYNDA BARRY © 1987

YARP YARP

IF YOU GO UP PAST THE SCHOOL, WAY UP PAST THE FIRE STATION, KEEP GOING, KEEP GOING, UNTIL YOU GET TO THAT YELLOW GAS STATION. IN THE PINK HOUSE NEXT TO IT, OUT IN THE YARD, IS A DOG WEARING CLOTHES.

OUR MOM SAYS MRS. SANTOS, THE LADY OF THE DOG, IS SO LONELY THAT THE DOG IS HER ONLY FAMILY. SHE TREATS PIXIE LIKE A REAL BABY FEEDING HIM SCRAMBLED EGGS WITH A TINY SPOON AND MAKING THE SAME FACES REGULAR MOMS MAKE WHEN THEY FEED REAL BABIES. ISN'T IT HEARTBREAKING, OUR MOM SAYS.

HERE COMES THE AIRPLANE!

"ISN'T IT HEARTBREAKING HOW SHE PUT A STATUE OF THE VIRGIN MARY AND A MILLION PLASTIC FLOWERS ON HIS DOGHOUSE? AND ALL THE PICTURES TAPED INSIDE, OF MOVIE STARS LIKE ROBERT MITCHUM? THAT DOG IS HER WHOLE LIFE, OUR MOM SAYS. SHE'D STARVE BEFORE SHE'D LET THAT DOG GO HUNGRY AND THAT DOG IS SO SPOILED. I'VE SEEN IT TRY TO BITE HER WHEN SHE GAVE IT A POWDER SUGAR DOUGHNUT. SHE WORSHIPS THAT DOG."

CHEF BOY-AR-DEE!

Pixie

UH-OH
SPAGETTI-O'S

"I FEEL SO SORRY FOR HER." SAID MOM. BUT WE FELT A LOT SORRIER FOR PIXIE WHO THREW UP ALL THE TIME AND WAS MRS. SANTOS'S THIRD DOG THIS YEAR.

YOO-HOO! ♪ PIXIE! ♪ HERE BOY! ♪ MOMMY HAS MORE CAKE AND ICE CREAM ♪ FOR HER LITTE BOO-BOO!

TRIXIE   DIXIE

ZOOM

the NEIGHBOR MAN

by LYNDA BARRY © 1985

CAN YOU COME OUT?

TO WHERE?

ONE MORNING LILA FROM ACROSS THE STREET CAME OVER AND ASKED ME DID I WANT TO COME WITH, SHE HAD TO GO DOWN TO THE A+P PARKING LOT TO LOOK FOR HER FATHER'S TEETH.

MR. PEARSON LOST HIS TEETH A LOT BECAUSE HE HATED HAVING THEM IN HIS MOUTH. SOMETIMES IF HE WAS REALLY MAD, HE'D THROW THEM. IF HE WAS JUST DRUNK, HE'D LAY THEM DOWN SOMEWHERE AND WALK AWAY. WE LOOKED ALL OVER THE PARKING LOT BUT HAD NO LUCK.

I GIVE.

SAME HERE, BUT I'LL GET CREAMED IF I DON'T FIND 'EM.

MAYBE THEY'RE AT THE BOWLING ALLEY

C'MON.

WE WENT INTO THE BOWLING ALLEY AND HAD A FIGHT OVER WHO HAD TO ASK. THEN A BALD MAN WALKED UP TO US REALLY FAST AND SAID "WHO ARE YOU HERE WITH?" WE SAID "NO ONE" AND HE SAID "THEN GO HOME, GET OUT!" THEN LILA FINALLY ASKED HIM ABOUT THE TEETH.

YOU PEARSON'S KID?

UH-HUH.

YEAH, BONNIE HAS 'EM IN THE LOUNGE.

YOUR DAD'S ONE SORRY SONNAVA BITCH, BOY.

WE HAD TO DIG THEM OUT OF A GARBAGE CAN. I COULD TELL THAT LILA WAS EMBARASSED. AT LEAST SHE WOULDN'T GET CREAMED. AT LEAST SHE FOUND THEM. WHEN WE GOT TO HER HOUSE HER DAD WAS LAYING ON THE COUCH. SHE TOLD ME TO GO WAIT ON THE PORCH.

HEY DAD? DAD?

WHAT IN TH' HELL...
GET THOSE DAMN THINGS OUT OF MY SIGHT!

MARLYS the STAR

BY LYNDA 8-TRACK TAPE BARRY ©1987

WHO KNOWS HOW IT HAPPENED BUT MARLYS GOT PICKED TO RIDE ON THE <u>FLOAT</u> IN THE <u>PARADE</u> WEARING A <u>UNIFORM</u>. WHEN MOM DROPPED US OFF, SHE HAD IT ON AND SHOUTED "ATEN-HUT!", "ABOUT FACE!", AND "YOU HAVE THE RIGHT TO REMAIN SILENT!". MY BROTHER SECRETLY GAVE HER THE FINGER AND SO DID I BECAUSE THE FACT IS WE WERE SO JEALOUS WE COULD DIE.

AFTER ABOUT A ZILLION YEARS OF WAITING, RIGHT WHEN YOUR BUTT IS DEAD FROM SITTING ON THE CURB, THE PARADE MEN COME RUNNING BY POINTING TO YOUR SHOES AND YELLING "MOVE THEM BACK! MOVE THEM OUT OF THE WAY!" AND BEFORE YOU KNOW IT A MILLION THINGS ARE GOING BY. THE BANDS ARE SO LOUD IT'S LIKE THEY'RE MARCHING ALL OVER YOU AND IF YOU SQUAT DOWN IT CAN BE PRETTY INTERES-TING TO WATCH THEIR FEET.

THE HORSE RIDERS GO BY, MORE BANDS GO BY, OUR PRINCIPAL AND ONE TEACHER FROM OUR SCHOOL AND THE JANITOR GO BY IN A GROUP OF DADS WEARING THEIR OLD ARMY UNIFORMS AND HATS AND MEDALS, THE BEAUTY CONTESTS GO BY SITTING ON THE BACKS OF CONVERTIBLES WAVING THEIR GLOVES AT YOU AND THE ONE CAR WITH THE QUEEN AND TWO PRINCESSES, HAS A GUY DRIVING IT WHO MY BROTHER BET ME A MILLION DOLLARS WAS DEAN MARTIN.

THE CLOWNS THREW THE WORST CANDY IN THE WORLD AT US AND WHEN THEY CAME UP TO GRAB YOU, YOU COULD SEE THEIR MAKE-UP AND THEY SMELLED DRUNK. THEN ALL OF A SUDDEN, HERE COMES THE FLOAT WITH MARLYS ON IT— AND BEFORE ME AND MY BROTHER KNEW WHAT WE WERE DOING WE STARTED YELLING "YAY MARLYS! YAY MARLYS!" AND SCREAMING, AND MARLYS DID THAT GLOVE WAVE JUST PERFECT AT US AND SHE STARTED LAUGHING AND WE STARTED LAUGHING AND I GUESS I'LL JUST NEVER FORGET THAT FOREVER.

MY FIRST LOVE

by Lynda "SHOUT BAMA-LAMA" Barris © 1985

MY FIRST LOVE WAS CALVIN IN ROOM 2, WHO I WILL NEVER FORGET. HE HAD BIG GLASSES THAT MADE HIS EYES ALL GIANT AND WACKY, LOOKING LIKE MY FISH SWIMMING UNDER WATER.

YOU COULD ALREADY TELL FROM HIS GLASSES WHAT A GENIUS, AND BESIDES THAT HE HAD A STUTTER WHICH I LOVED TO LISTEN TO. NO ONE I EVER MET COULD TALK LIKE THAT. I TRIED IT AT HOME BUT MY MOM YELLED CAN IT. DID I WANT TO GROW UP RETARDED?!

SHE WAS TALKIN' LIKE THAT BOY AGAIN MOM. BUT I WAS TALKIN' PERFECT.

I WOULD SIT ON THE FRONT PORCH AND PICK THE PAINT OFF THE STEPS, THINKING ONLY OF HIM. THERE WAS A GOOD SONG ON THE RADIO FOR IT, AND I WOULD SING IT OVER AND OVER AND IMAGINE CALVIN IN HIS PAJAMAS.

CU-PID DRAW BAKYER BOW-OH ANN LET YOUR ARRA FLOW-OH STRAIGHT TO MAH LOVERS HAART FOR MEE. CUPID DRAW BACK AN LET CHER ARRA TO MA LOVERS HEART FOR ME CUPID DRAW AN LET Y MY LOU

ONE TIME ME AND CALVIN WERE WALKING THE SAME WAY AND I TOLD HIM WOULD HE MARRY ME. HE SAID O.K. THEN WE WALKED BY OLD MRS. MITCHELL'S AND I TOLD HER CALVIN AND I WERE GOING TO GET MARRIED. SHE POINTED HER FINGER AT ME AND SAID "STAY AWAY FROM NEGRO BOYS, CHILD! THEY BEAT WHITE WOMEN!" WHICH WAS DUMB BECAUSE I WAS A <u>LOT</u> FASTER THAN CALVIN.

NUH-UH MRS. ROSE CALVIN CAN'T RACE THAT GOOD!

THEN I FOUND OUT FROM THESE GIRLS
THAT IT WAS EMBARASSING TO LIKE
CALVIN. THIS WAS WAY BEFORE WE
LEARNED THE CONCEPT OF EVERY-
THING IS BEAUTIFUL IN ITS OWN WAY
(WHICH HARDLY ANYONE EVER BELIEVED).
    THEY TOLD ME IF I WANTED THE
GIRLS TO LIKE ME I HAD TO KNOCK OFF
LIKING CALVIN. I HAD NO CHOICE.

WE DON'T
LIKE ANYONE
WHO PLAYS
WITH
SPAZ-MOS.

I HAD TO SAY "YOU ARE A CRUDDY
FISH-EY·ES, CA-CA-CA-CA-CALVIN"
RIGHT TO HIS FACE TO PROVE I
HATED HIM. AND THE FUNNY THING
ABOUT IT WAS HOW HE LOOKED RIGHT
BACK AT ME LIKE I WASN'T SAYING
ANYTHING BIG.

HOWZ YER
BUH-BUH-BUH
BUH-BOYFRIEND
DOIN', HUH?

SHUT UP!

TOM'S MOM

BY LYNDA THE Cutter BARRY © 1986

FIRST TOM'S MOM WAS A REGULAR MOM, THEN SHE GOT SKINNY, THEN SHE WAS IN THE HOSPITAL, THEN SHE WAS IN THE HOSPITAL AGAIN AND TOM STAYED AT OUR HOUSE A LONG TIME, THEN THE DAY HIS DAD CAME TO GET HIM CAME, AND THE SAD PART ABOUT IT WAS, WELL, YOU KNOW.

THANK YOU EVELYN.

COME ON SON.

I'M SO SORRY BILL. CALL IF YOU NEED ANYTHING

BYE YA TOM

BYE YA MARTY I'LL CALL YOU UP OK?

OK.

THEN I DIDN'T SEE TOM FOR A WHOLE WEEK, HE DIDN'T COME TO SCHOOL OR NOTHING. THEN HE COMES TO OUR HOUSE WAY TOO EARLY IN THE MORNING ON A BIKE THAT'S NOT EVEN HIS. A GIRL'S BIKE. AND HE WANTS TO KNOW CAN I COME OUT. MOM SAYS O.K. BUT EAT SOMETHING FIRST. TOM SAID HE ALREADY ATE BUT I KNOW HE'S LYING. HE LOOKS LIKE HE AIN'T ATE IN ABOUT A YEAR.

I KNOW IT'S SAD TOMMY, BUT YOUR MAMA IS A LOT HAPPIER NOW. SHE'S BEEN CALLED UP TO HEAVEN HONEY. SHE'S ONE OF GOD'S ANGELS WATCHING OVER YOU.

YEAH. AND SHE PROBABLY GOT A RIDE TO HEAVEN ON A FLYING CARPET. AND SHE CAN FLY AND TURN INVISIBLE.

RIGHT MOM?

WHEN WE GOT OUTSIDE TOM SLUGGED ME ON THE ARM AND SAID IF I EVER SAID ONE MORE WORD ABOUT HIS MOM HE WOULD KILL ME. NORMALLY I WOULD HAVE SLUGGED HIM BACK BUT THIS TIME I JUST DIDN'T. HE WANTED ME TO COME OVER TO THE GRAVEYARD TO SEE WHERE HIS MOM WAS. TO GO OVER THERE BY OURSELVES. I ABOUT STARTED CRYING RIGHT THEN. I GOT OUT MY BIKE AND WE WERE RIDING AND I WAS HOPING THEY DIDN'T LET NO KIDS WITH BIKES IN THERE.

NOBODY STOPPED US. WE DROVE PAST ABOUT A MILLION GRAVES TIL WE CAME TO HIS MOM'S. WE GOT OFF OUR BIKES AND COULDN'T EVEN SAY NOTHING. FINALLY TOM STARTS SAYING THE PLEDGE OF ALLEGIANCE AND I SAY IT WITH HIM. BY THE END OF IT WELL WE ARE CRYING.

WHEN WE GET BACK TO MY HOUSE TOM DOES THIS WEIRD THING. MY MOM'S WATCHING T.V. AND TOM GOES OVER THERE AND SITS ON HER LAP LIKE HE'S A BABY. MOM PUTS HER ARMS AROUND HIM LIKE IT'S NO BIG DEAL AND THEN WE ALL SIT THERE WATCHING SOME SHOW I CAN'T EVEN REMEMBER.

NO BIG DEAL

BY LYNDA "SLEEPTALKIN'" BARRY ©1986

OUT OF ALL THE GIRLS IN OUR CLASS, IT WAS ONLY ONE GIRL WHO DIDN'T GET NO INVITATION TO MARISSA BATO'S BIRTHDAY PARTY. I GUESS SHE FIGURED WE WOULD ALL NEED ONE GIRL TO BRAG ABOUT THE PARTY TO. THE GIRL WHO WASN'T INVITED WAS MY COUSIN MARLYS.

HOW COME? HOW COME YOU DIDN'T INVITE ME?

UH... MY MOM SAID I COULD ONLY HAVE 13 GIRLS COME.

EVEN THOUGH ME AND MARLYS WERE TOTAL HATERS OF EACH OTHER, I FELT SORRY THAT SHE DIDN'T GET A INVITATION. AT LUNCH I WENT OVER TO HER TABLE TO NOTICE HER FEELINGS.

QUIT STARIN' AT ME, STUPE!

IT'S A FREE COUNTRY.

WHO EVEN CARES ABOUT MARISSA'S PARTY? I DON'T CARE ABOUT THAT DUMB PARTY. IT'S NO BIG DEAL TO ME EVEN ONE BIT, SO WHO CARES?

IT'S AT A RESTAURANT.

I WOULDN'T GO FOR ALL THE MONEY IN THE WORLD. THERE'S NO WAY I'D EVER GO TO THAT STUPID PARTY.

IT'S AT BIG TOP ICE CREAM LAND.

MILK

IT TURNS OUT THE DAY BEFORE THE PARTY I GOT THE FLU. MARLYS IS OVER JUMPING UP AND DOWN TO TAKE MY INVITATION. I KNEW FOR A FACT MARISSA DIDN'T WANT NO MARLYS AT HER PARTY BUT I HAD TO GIVE HER MY INVITATION BECAUSE MY MOM WOULDN'T LISTEN TO ME WHEN I TRIED TO EXPLAIN IT. SHE SAID I WAS JUST TRYING TO BE MEAN.

MOM, YOU DON'T GET IT.

DON'T YOU DARE TALK TO ME THAT WAY YOU SELFISH CHILD! YOU OUGHT TO BE ASHAMED OF YOURSELF!

I'VE HAD QUITE ENOUGH OF YOUR SELF-CENTEREDNESS!

BUT NOT GIVING HER THAT INVITATION WOULDN'T HAVE BEEN HALF AS MEAN AS WHAT MARISSA DID TO HER.

WHO CARES ABOUT MARISSA BATOS ANYWAY? SHE'S A STUPID IDIOT.

SHE WOULDN'T EVEN TAKE MY PRESENT.

BOYS. LIFE.

ONE DAY ME AND DEENA WERE SITTING UP ON THE PORCH WAITING FOR OUR REQUEST TO BE PLAYED ON "KOLORFUL KOL, CH. 95", WHEN WE SAW ALL THE BOYS WALKING IN A LINE THIS CERTAIN WAY.

IT WAS PIMP WALKING AND YOU HAD TO PRACTICE AT IT TO BE ANY GOOD. EVERY BOY PRACTICED IT ALL SUMMER ESPECIALLY IF THEY MADE A GOOD PLAY IN KICK BALL. IF YOU DID A GOOD ANYTHING HOW YOU SHOWED IT WAS BY A PIMP WALK. IF A GIRL DID IT THOUGH, NOBODY LIKED THAT.

THE BEST PIMP WALKER OF ALL WAS GARY KINOHARA WHICH MADE EVERYBODY MAD. THEY SAID IT DON'T LOOK RIGHT HAVING A JAPANESE PIMPING, BUT EVERYONE KNEW HE WAS BEST BECAUSE WHEN HE STARTED DOING IT WE ALL WOULD JUST NATURALLY SHUT UP IN AWE OF HIM. BUT <u>NOBODY</u> WOULD ALLOW HIM TO LEAD THE LINE. YOU COULDN'T WALK BEHIND NO JAPANESE.

WHERE THE BOYS WERE HEADED WAS UP TO THE SCHOOL AND WHEN THEY GOT ONTO THE PLAYFIELD THEY SAW ANDREA AND HER BAD SISTER CAROL AND SO THEY REALLY STARTED PIMPING HARD AND THEY SAID A TERRIBLE CHANT ABOUT ANDREA.

THE LEADER OF THE LINE WAS RICKY WHO WAS ANDREA'S BOYFRIEND. HE WAS THE ONE WHO WOULD YELL OUT THE CHANT AND THE OTHER GUYS WOULD DO THE BACKGROUND. THEY MARCHED RIGHT UP TO ANDREA'S FACE AND CAROL YELLS "COME ON LET'S GET AWAY FROM THESE FOOLS" BUT ANDREA JUST LOOKS STRAIGHT AT RICKY, STANDING THERE LIKE SHE'S PARALIZED.

I SAID OOH - AH. OOH. UH. AH. UH. I SAID OOH - AH. OOH. UH. AH.

I SAY TO DEENA WE HAD BETTER GO GET SOMEONE'S MOM BUT DEENA SAYS IT'S NOT WORTH IT. SHE SAYS THEY AREN'T GOING TO HIT ANDREA OR NOTHING. THEY ARE JUST PAYING HER BACK FOR KISSING WITH A BUNCH OF THEM IN THE GARAGE.

LET'S GO! C'MON MAN! QUIT STARIN' OR THEY'LL CREAM US.

BAD CHILDREN

BY LYNDA BARRY © 1986

ON OUR BLOCK THERE WERE THE GOOD CHILDREN AND THERE WERE THE BAD CHILDREN. THEY WERE EASY TO TELL APART. THE GOOD ONES COULD NEVER HARDLY COME OUTSIDE AND THE BAD ONES WERE OUT ALL THE TIME BREAKING STUFF.

A LOT OF TIMES BAD CHILDREN CAME IN WHOLE FAMILIES ALTHOUGH THEY COULD BE BAD IN DIFFERENT WAYS. SOME WERE BAD IN THE WAY THEY WOULD JUST SOCK YOU FOR NO REASON AND YELL SWEARS AT ANYONE, EVEN THEIR OWN PARENTS. TO ME, THEY WERE THE SCARYEST.

THEN THERE WERE THE ONES WHO WERE JUST ALWAYS IN A BAD MOOD AND NEVER SAID NOTHING BUT BAD THINGS TO EVERYONE AND NEVER CRIED ABOUT NOTHING EVEN IF THEIR DOG GOT RUN OVER.

THERE WERE ONES WHO WERE BAD SPORTS, WHO WERE BAD AT EVERYTHING THEY DID, WHO CRIED EVEN IF YOU DIDN'T DO NOTHING TO THEM AND WHO ALWAYS TOLD. EVERYONE HATED THEM, EVEN TEACHERS.

HOW COME YOU LOOK SO STUPID?

I'M GOIN' TA JANETTE RHINEHOLT'S BIRTHDAY PARTY. SHE SAYS YOU WOULDA GOT INVITED EXCEPT HER MOM SAID SHE COULD ONLY INVITE 24 GIRLS.

BIG DEAL. I WOULDN'TA GONE IF SHE BEGGED ME AND YOU'RE STUPID FOR GOIN' TOO.

WHY LOOK CLASS, RENEE IS GIVING US ANOTHER PERFORMANCE THIS AFTERNOON! LETS ALL STAND UP AND GIVE HER A BIG HAND FOR HER SUPERB ACTING!

MY DAD KNOWS THE PRESIDENT AND HE'S GONNA PUT YOU IN JAIL FOR THIS MISS BURR.

SO YOU BETTER BE NICER TO ME. YOU BETTER.

BUT IN ALMOST EVERY BAD FAMILY THERE WAS ALWAYS ONE WHO ACTED GOOD IN ALMOST EVERY WAY. THEY DID O.K. IN SCHOOL, THEY WERE NEVER MEAN, THEY WEREN'T CRY-BABIES BUT THEY HARDLY EVER LAUGHED NEITHER. THE MAIN THING ABOUT THEM WAS THEY ALWAYS KNEW WHAT TIME IT WAS AND THEY TOOK CARE OF THEIR BROTHERS AND SISTERS.

COME ON YOU GUYS! DINNER! COME ON!

RENEE GO FIND THE LITTLE ONES.

MAKE ME!

WHO WANTS TA EAT YOUR LOUSY COOKIN?

THE ONLY WAY THEY WERE BAD WAS JUST BY FEELING IT.

YOU TELL THOSE GUYS TA QUIET DOWN OR THEY'LL WAKE UP MOM!!

THEY AIN'T GONNA WAKE UP MOM CAUSE SHE DON'T WAKE UP WHEN SHES DRUNK.

WHERES HER PURSE?

FORGET IT.

WHERED YOU HIDE HER PURSE OR I'LL BEAT YOUR ASS.

FISHFACE

BY LYNDA PYRAMID POWER BARRY © 1986

I GOT THE NAME FISHFACE BY THIS ONE GIRL AND THE WORST PART ABOUT IT IS I USTA LIKE HER. I LIKED HER, THE GIRL WHO RUINED MY ENTIRE LIFE. BUT ONE THING I CAN SAY FOR HER, SHE WAS GOOD AT MAKING UP NAMES.

SAY IT RENEE. I DARE YA. TELL HIM THE NAME YOU SAID FOR HIM.

SHOULD I?

YEAH! DONNY DON'T CARE. SAY IT! ITS JUST FOR FUN.

SHE ALWAYS HAD SOMETHING SMART TO SAY TO EVERYONE. EVEN TEACHERS. SO A LOT OF TIMES DURING RECESS YOU'D SEE HER SITTING IN THE OFFICE PICKING HER NAILS AND PROBABLY THINKING UP MORE NAMES FOR PEOPLE.

RENEE, ARE YOU READY TO GO BACK OUTSIDE AND BE A GOOD CITIZEN?

NOPE.

O.K. THEN. I GUESS YOU'LL JUST HAVE TO SIT THERE UNTIL YOU DO DECIDE TO BE A GOOD CITIZEN.

FINE WITH ME MRS. STINK BALL.

THEN ONE DAY I HAD TO GO TO THE SEARS WITH MY MOM AND WE PARK RIGHT NEXT TO A CAR WITH RENEE SITTING IN IT. WHEN SHE SEES ME SHE DUCKS HER HEAD SO IT LOOKS LIKE THE CAR IS JUST EMPTY. I DON'T KNOW WHY SHE DOES THAT. I DON'T KNOW WHY SHE DOESN'T YELL OUT THE WINDOW "HIYA FISHFACE! HOW YA DOIN' FISH FACE!" THEN I SEE THIS LADY START TO OPEN THE DOOR OF RENEE'S CAR AND SHE IS HOLDING THE HAND OF AN ACTUAL RETARDED. IT'S RENEE'S MOM. WITH I GUESS HER BROTHER. MY MOM YANKS MY ARM. "DON'T STARE!" SHE WHISPERS.

DONALD!

THE NEXT DAY AT SCHOOL RENEE PASSES IT AROUND THAT "WHATEVER FISH FACE SAYS IS A LIE". I DIDN'T EVEN SAY ANYTHING. AFTER THAT, RENEE HATED ME HARDER THAN SHE HATED ANYBODY. BUT THE WEIRDEST PART OF ALL WAS, THAT WAS WHEN I REALLY STARTED LOVING HER.

I HATE YOU! I HATE YOU! I WISH YOU WERE DEAD!

I'M NOT GONNA TELL RENEE. I'M NEVER GONNA TELL NO ONE.

SHUT-UP! SHUT-UP!

WALKING HOME

BY LYNDA "RUBBER HEAD" BARRY ©1986

I HAD SOME FRIENDS WHO WEREN'T EXACTLY THE GOODEST GUYS IN THE WORLD. MY MOM HATED THEM WHICH WAS PRETTY BAD BECAUSE ONE OF THEM WAS MY OTHER BROTHER HENRY WHO HAD TO LIVE WITH MY DAD. SOMETIMES SHE WOULDN'T EVEN LET HIM COME IN THE HOUSE.

DON'T LOOK AT ME THAT WAY A.J. HENRY HAS HIS OWN HOUSE, CORRECT? HE MADE HIS DECISION TO LIVE WITH HIS FATHER SO HE CAN GO PLAY IN HIS OWN HOUSE.

YEAH, BUT I CAN'T GO OVER THERE, SO HOW ARE ME AND HENRY SUPPOSED TO GET TO EVEN DO ANYTHING?

WHY DON'T YOU PLAY WITH YOUR BROTHER ALEC?

MOM, ALECS A BABY, MAN!

I WASN'T SUPPOSED TO GO OVER TO MY DAD'S BECAUSE OF THAT LADY MY DAD GOT MARRIED TO, BUT WHO WANTED TO ANYHOW SINCE SHE HATED MY GUTS PLUS HENRY'S GUTS ALSO. SHE HAD A NEW BABY NAMED MELLIE AND HENRY AND ME BOTH HATED THAT BABY'S GUTS. SO MOSTLY ME AND HENRY JUST SAW EACH OTHER WALKING HOME. ME AND HENRY HARDLY EVER LIKED EACH OTHER UNTIL EVERYTHING GOT SCREWED UP. THEN ALL OF A SUDDEN WE LIKED EACH OTHER SO MUCH YOU COULDN'T HARDLY TELL WE WERE BROTHERS.

WHAT DO YOU WANT TO DO OLD CHAP?

I DON'T KNOW. WHAT DO YOU WANT TO DO MY GOOD FELLOW?

I DON'T KNOW, WHAT DO YOU WANT TO DO JEEVES?

I DON'T KNOW, WHAT DO YOU WHAT TO DO QUIGLEY?

IN THE SUMMER WE WOULD SNEAK OUT IN THE MIDDLE OF THE NIGHT AND MEET ON UPPER FIELD UP AT THE SCHOOL. WE'D CLIMB UP ONTO THE ROOF OF THE SCHOOL AND STAND BY THE EDGE WITH OUR ARMS HOLDED OUT SAYING STUFF LIKE "GOOD-BYE CRUEL WORLD" AND "I AM THE KING OF THE ENTIRE UNIVERSE." IF MY MOM EVER KNEW SHE WOULD HAVE KILLED ME. HENRY SAID DAD WOULDN'T HAVE EVEN CARED. HENRY AND ME WROTE OUR NAMES UP THERE ONE NIGHT WITH BLUE SPRAY PAINT IN A PLACE YOU COULD ONLY SEE IF YOU CLIMBED-UP.

THEN WHEN MOM MOVED US TO ANOTHER TOWN TO GO LIVE WITH GRANDMA I SWORE ON THE BIBLE TO HENRY I'D COME BACK. BUT I NEVER CAME BACK. I'LL BET YOU ANYTHING HE USED TO CLIMB ONTO THE ROOF AT THE SCHOOL SOMETIMES AND JUST LOOK AT OUR NAMES AND JUST HATE MY GUTS.

INBARASSMINT

LYNDA "THE LONELY BULL" BARRY © 1986

ROLANDO HAD A MOM THAT LIKED TO COME TO PARTIES. HIS DAD HAD PASSED AWAY AFTER A TREE FELL ON HIM ONCE. ROLANDO SAID IT WAS THE WORST DAY OF HIS LIFE WHEN THAT THE DOCTOR CAME OUT OF THE OPERATION LOOKING SO SORRY. ROLANDO WOULD NEVER WATCH MARCUS WELBY.

ON NEW YEAR'S EVE THE PARTY WAS AT OUR HOUSE IN THE BASEMENT. ROLANDO'S MOM CAME FIRST WITH ROLANDO ALREADY IN HIS PAJAMAS. MOM MADE US T.V. DINNERS AND MADE US PROMISE TWO THINGS: BE GOOD AND STAY UPSTAIRS. WE SAID O.K. THEN OUR TWO MOMS HAD THEM SOME HIGH BALLS AND WAITED FOR MY DAD TO GET BACK.

PRETTY SOON WE COULD HARDLY EVEN HEAR THE T.V. FROM ALL THE NOISE IN THE BASEMENT. ROLANDO SAID HE THOUGHT THEY WERE DOING THE MEXICAN HAT DANCE AND LET'S GO SNEAK SOME LOOKS OFFA THE STAIRS. I SAID O.K. AND WE WENT LIKE I-SPY. SURE ENOUGH THEY WERE!

I COULD SEE MY MOM AND MY DAD BUT I COULDN'T SEE ROLANDO'S MOM NOWHERE. WE LOOKED A LONG TIME AND I COULD TELL HE WAS GETTING THAT SICK FEELING OF WHERE WAS SHE. I SAID WE BETTER GO BACK UP-STAIRS AND HE SAID YEAH WE BETTER. WHEN WE PASSED THROUGH THE KITCHEN WE BOTH SAW HER OUT ON THE PATIO LAUGHING AND OPENING HER SHIRT TO A MAN.

WE WENT UP TO MY ROOM AND JUST SAT THERE. I ASKED ROLANDO DID HE WANT TO PLAY SOMETHING. HE SAID "I DON'T CARE." I ASKED HIM DID HE WANT TO MESS AROUND WITH MY MONSTER MODELS. HE SAID "I DON'T CARE."

WHICH DO YA WANNA BE, FRANKENSTEIN OR THE MUMMY? YOU CAN HAVE FIRST PICK.

I DON'T CARE

THEN HE SAYS REAL LOUD "THAT LADY WASN'T MY MOM YOU KNOW." AND HE LOOKS AT ME LIKE I'M ABOUT TO CALL HIM A LIAR OR SOMETHING.

A FUNNY NIGHT

BY LYNDA "HUGGA BUTT" BARRY © 1986

IT WAS A FUNNY NIGHT AND EVERYONE KNEW IT. ACROSS THE STREET THEY WERE BEING SO NICE AND LAUGHING WITH EACH OTHER ON THE PORCH, AND AT OUR HOUSE, WELL, WE WERE DOING THE SAME THING. EVERYONE'S DAD WAS HOME. NO ONE'S MOM WAS MAD. THEN FRAN SHOWS UP WITH ABOUT 20 HAMBURGERS LEFT OVER FROM HIS JOB.

MY SISTER WAS SECRETLY IN LOVE WITH FRAN SO SHE'S THE FIRST ONE TO RUN DOWN THE STAIRS AND INTO THE STREET. PRETTY SOON EVERYONE'S DOWN THERE WATCHING FRAN LINE UP THE HAMBURGERS ON THE HOOD OF THE CAR SAYING DON'T TOUCH 'EM 'TIL I SAY. MY DAD HAS HIS ARM AROUND MY MOM AND FRAN'S MOM AND DAD ARE DOING THE SAME WHICH MAKES ALL US KIDS LOOK AT EACH OTHER AND TRY TO BE ESPECIALLY GOOD SO THAT NOTHING WILL STOP.

FRAN'S MOM SAYS WHO WANTS TO GO IN THE BASEMENT AND BRING UP SOME POP AND WE ALL YELL "I DO!" EVERYONE KNOWS POP IS EXPENSIVE SO WE JUST TAKE ONE EACH AND NOBODY GOES AND HIDES EXTRA ONES IN THE BUSHES FOR LATER. NOT TONIGHT. FRAN'S DAD AND OUR DAD BOTH OPEN ALL THE CANS AND THEN EVERYBODY TAKES A HAMBURGER AND WE ALL WATCH EACH OTHER AND LAUGH AT ANYTHING. EVERY ONCE IN A WHILE ONE OF THE LITTLE ONES WILL GET TOO EXCITED AND START DOING A DANCE.

THEN EVERYONE GOES OVER TO FRAN'S PORCH AND OUR MOM AND DAD AND THEIR MOM AND DAD TALK AND WE'RE RACING UP AND DOWN THE BLOCK AT LEAST 10 THOUSAND TIMES. THEY KEPT TALKING EVEN AFTER WE QUIT AND I ENDED UP KONKING OUT ON THE GRASS. I WOKE UP JUST IN TIME TO KEEP PRE- TENDING I WAS ASLEEP WHEN MY DAD PICKED ME UP TO CARRY ME BACK HOME.

This book is dedicated to my little brothers with deep love, and to the memory of our dog, Fidjer.

Mark

Michael